Link Reversal Algorithms

Synthesis Lectures on Distributed Computing Theory

Editor
Nancy Lynch, *Massachusetts Institute of Technology*

Synthesis Lectures on Distributed Computing Theory is edited by Nancy Lynch of the Massachusetts Institute of Technology. The series will publish 50- to 150 page publications on topics pertaining to distributed computing theory. The scope will largely follow the purview of premier information and computer science conferences, such as ACM PODC, DISC, SPAA, OPODIS, CONCUR, DialM-POMC, ICDCS, SODA, Sirocco, SSS, and related conferences. Potential topics include, but not are limited to: distributed algorithms and lower bounds, algorithm design methods, formal modeling and verification of distributed algorithms, and concurrent data structures.

Link Reversal Algorithms
Jennifer L. Welch and Jennifer E. Walter
2011

Cooperative Task-Oriented Computing: Algorithms and Complexity
Chryssis Georgiou, Alexander A. Shvartsman
2011

New Models for Population Protocols
Othon Michail, Ioannis Chatzigiannakis, Paul G. Spirakis
2011

The Theory of Timed I/O Automata, Second Edition
Dilsun K. Kaynar, Nancy Lynch, Roberto Segala, Frits Vaandrager
2010

Principles of Transactional Memory
Rachid Guerraoui, Michal Kapalka
2010

Fault-tolerant Agreement in Synchronous Message-passing Systems
Michel Raynal
2010

Communication and Agreement Abstractions for Fault-Tolerant Asynchronous Distributed Systems
Michel Raynal
2010

The Mobile Agent Rendezvous Problem in the Ring
Evangelos Kranakis, Danny Krizanc, Euripides Markou
2010

Link Reversal Algorithms

Jennifer L. Welch and Jennifer E. Walter

ISBN:978-3-031-00878-8   paperback
ISBN:978-3-031-02006-3   ebook

DOI 10.1007/978-3-031-02006-3

A Publication in the Springer series
SYNTHESIS LECTURES ON DISTRIBUTED COMPUTING THEORY

Lecture #8
Series Editor: Nancy Lynch, *Massachusetts Institute of Technology*
Series ISSN
Synthesis Lectures on Distributed Computing Theory
Print 2155-1626   Electronic 2155-1634

Link Reversal Algorithms

Jennifer L. Welch
Texas A&M University

Jennifer E. Walter
Vassar College

SYNTHESIS LECTURES ON DISTRIBUTED COMPUTING THEORY #8

ABSTRACT

Link reversal is a versatile algorithm design technique that has been used in numerous distributed algorithms for a variety of problems. The common thread in these algorithms is that the distributed system is viewed as a graph, with vertices representing the computing nodes and edges representing some other feature of the system (for instance, point-to-point communication channels or a conflict relationship). Each algorithm assigns a virtual direction to the edges of the graph, producing a directed version of the original graph. As the algorithm proceeds, the virtual directions of some of the links in the graph change in order to accomplish some algorithm-specific goal. The criterion for changing link directions is based on information that is local to a node (such as the node having no outgoing links) and thus this approach scales well, a feature that is desirable for distributed algorithms.

This monograph presents, in a tutorial way, a representative sampling of the work on link-reversal-based distributed algorithms. The algorithms considered solve routing, leader election, mutual exclusion, distributed queueing, scheduling, and resource allocation. The algorithms can be roughly divided into two types, those that assume a more abstract graph model of the networks, and those that take into account more realistic details of the system. In particular, these more realistic details include the communication between nodes, which may be through asynchronous message passing, and possible changes in the graph, for instance, due to movement of the nodes.

We have not attempted to provide a comprehensive survey of all the literature on these topics. Instead, we have focused in depth on a smaller number of fundamental papers, whose common thread is that link reversal provides a way for nodes in the system to observe their local neighborhoods, take only local actions, and yet cause global problems to be solved. We conjecture that future interesting uses of link reversal are yet to be discovered.

KEYWORDS

link reversal, distributed algorithms, routing, leader election, mutual exclusion, distributed queueing, scheduling, and resource allocation

Contents

Acknowledgments

We thank the authors of the fascinating papers surveyed in this monograph. We also thank our collaborators on link reversal research from whom we have learned a great deal: Guangtong Cao, Bernadette Charron-Bost, Matthias Függer, Antoine Gaillard, Rebecca Ingram, Savita Kini, Navneet Malpani, Nicholas Neumann, Evelyn Pierce, Tsvetomira Radeva, Patrick Shields, Nitin Vaidya, Saira Viqar, and Josef Widder. We are especially grateful to Nancy Lynch, Mira Radeva, Michel Raynal, and Josef Widder for carefully reading earlier drafts and providing helpful comments. J. Welch was supported in part by NSF grants 0500265 and 0964696, and Texas Higher Education Coordinating Board grants ARP 00512-0007-2006 and 00512-0130-2007. J. Walter was supported in part by NSF grant 0712911.

Jennifer L. Welch and Jennifer E. Walter
November 2011

CHAPTER 1

Introduction

Link reversal is a versatile algorithm design technique that has been used in numerous distributed algorithms for a variety of problems, including routing, leader election, mutual exclusion, distributed queueing, and resource allocation. The common thread in these algorithms is that the distributed system is viewed as a graph, with vertices representing the computing nodes and edges representing some other feature of the system (for instance, point-to-point communication channels or a conflict relationship). Each algorithm assigns a virtual direction to the edges of the graph, producing a directed version of the original graph with vertices and links. As the algorithm proceeds, the virtual directions of some of the links change in order to accomplish some algorithm-specific goal. The criterion for changing link directions is based on information that is local to a node (such as the node having no outgoing links) and thus this approach scales well, a feature that is desirable for distributed algorithms. To the best of our knowledge, the earliest published work proposing the concept of link reversal for distributed algorithms is that of Gafni and Bertsekas in 1981 [19].

This book presents, in a tutorial way, a representative sampling of the work on link-reversal-based distributed algorithms. These papers can be roughly divided into two types, those that assume a more abstract graph model of the networks, and those that take into account more realistic details of the system. In particular, these more realistic details include the communication between nodes, which may be through asynchronous message passing, and possible changes in the graph, for instance, due to movement of the nodes.

Section 2 begins our tour with the routing problem in a graph. For this situation, the graph represents the communication topology of a distributed system which contains a unique node, called the destination, to whom the other nodes in the system need to route messages. The goal is to assign directions to the edges of the topology graph that can be used to forward messages so that they are guaranteed to arrive at the destination. We present a suite of related algorithms for this problem, all of which assume that the graph is static and nodes have instantaneous access to the local states of their neighbors. The key idea in all these algorithms is that a vertex other than the destination that becomes a sink (all its incident links are incoming) causes some or all of its incident links to reverse direction; the algorithms differ in the choice of which links to reverse and how the reversal is implemented. First, we present the Full and Partial Reversal algorithms and their implementations based on assigning unbounded labels (called heights) to the graph vertices; this work is by Gafni and Bertsekas [19]. Then, we describe a different way of implementing Full and Partial Reversal, due to Charron-Bost et al. [11], that assigns binary labels to the graph links.

In Section 3, we characterize the work complexity and time complexity of these graph algorithms based on the work by Busch et al. [4, 5] and by Charron-Bost et al. [9, 10, 11, 12]. The work complexity counts the number of reversals done by the vertices while the time complexity measures the number of iterations that are required. The results presented include both worst-case bounds (i.e., what is the maximum value of work or time complexity in the most adversarial graph) and exact characterizations of the work and time complexity of an arbitrary vertex in an arbitrary graph. We compare the behavior of Full Reversal and Partial Reversal with respect to these two complexity measures using, in part, concepts from game theory.

In Section 4, we look at algorithms that have applied the more abstract ideas of link reversal routing in a graph to distributed systems that experience asynchronous message passing and topology changes. First, a routing algorithm called TORA that was designed for mobile ad hoc networks by Park and Corson [35] is described; it extends the height-based implementation of Partial Reversal to handle the problem of network partitions. Then extensions of TORA for the related problem of electing a leader in a mobile ad hoc network by Malapni et al. [31] and Ingram et al. [26] are discussed. The key idea here is that the destination node can be considered the leader of its connected component; when a partition is detected using the TORA mechanism, a new leader needs to be elected in the partitioned component.

In the mutual exclusion problem [17], nodes contend for exclusive access to a shared resource; each node that requires access should eventually be granted (exclusive) access to the resource. Link reversal ideas have been used to ensure mutual exclusion in distributed systems. Section 5 describes one such algorithm, due to Snepscheut [40], and proves that it is correct, using ideas from Raymond [38] and Walter et al. [42]. In the algorithm, access to the shared resource is only allowed when a node possesses a unique token, which is sent around the network in messages. An invariant of the algorithm is that the links are always directed toward the location of the token in the system. When the token is sent over a communication channel, the corresponding link reverses direction to maintain the invariant. In contrast to the routing algorithms, at certain times a node makes itself become a sink; these times are when the node is in its so-called "critical section" using the shared resource.

Distributed mutual exclusion solutions that provide some level of fair access to the shared resource are essentially implementing a kind of distributed queue. A distributed queue is useful in other applications as well. Demmer and Herlihy [15] abstracted the distributed queueing aspect from Raymond's spanning-tree-based algorithm as the Arrow protocol, and showed how it is useful for implementing a distributed directory. In Section 6, following Herlihy et al. [23], we describe the Arrow protocol and prove that it is correct in a system with static topology and asynchronous message delays.

Going back to the problem of routing in a graph using Full Reversal, Section 7 studies what happens if there is no destination, in other words, if *all* vertices that are sinks reverse all their incident links. It turns out that the existence of a vertex that never does a reversal (the destination) is crucial for ensuring that Full Reversal terminates. Without such a node, the algorithm never terminates, and in fact every vertex does an infinite number of reversals. We can view the times when a vertex is a sink as times when the vertex is *scheduled* to take some kind of action; by the notion of being a sink, it is guaranteed that two neighboring nodes are never scheduled simultaneously, so the algorithm provides an exclusion property. The bulk of this section is devoted to analyzing the *concurrency* of the algorithm (during what fraction of the iterations is any given vertex scheduled), as a function of the input graph. This work was done by Barbosa and Gafni [2].

Section 8 applies link reversal ideas for scheduling to the resource allocation problem in distributed systems. Consider a network with a static communication topology and asynchronous message passing, in which the nodes cycle through waiting for access to a shared resource, using the shared resource, and being uninterested in the shared resource. Each resource is shared between two nodes and a "conflict graph" that is a subgraph of the communication topology describes the pattern of sharing. Chandy and Misra [7] designed an algorithm in which every node that wants to use the shared resource eventually gets exclusive access to the resource. In this algorithm, a directed version of the conflict graph is used to break ties between contending neighbors; this graph is updated using Full Reversal: when a node finishes using the resource, it reverses all its incident links in the conflict graph to be outgoing, so as to give priority to all its neighbors. One difference from Full Reversal routing is that non-sink nodes can sometimes do a reversal: Because of a desire not to involve nodes that have no interest in using the shared resource, a node that is not a sink may be able to use the resource, and then when it finishes it reverses its incident links. This section presents the algorithm together with a correctness proof.

We conclude in Section 9, having presented a number of different distributed applications for which link reversal is a natural solution as well as a variety of proof techniques for correctness and complexity of the algorithms underlying these applications.

CHAPTER 2

Routing in a Graph: Correctness

In this section, we consider a graph that represents the communication topology of a distributed system which contains a unique node, called the destination, to whom the other nodes in the system need to route messages. In Section 2.1, we begin with the necessary graph-theoretic definitions, define the routing problem, describe a generic version of a routing algorithm based on link reversal, and present two important specializations of the generic algorithm, Full Reversal and Partial Reversal. Section 2.2 focuses on implementations of the generic algorithm that assign unbounded labels to the vertices of the graph, while Section 2.3 covers implementations that assign binary labels to the links of the graph. The focus here is on showing the correctness of the algorithms, namely, that they terminate with link directions that enable routing to the destination.

2.1   ABSTRACT LINK REVERSAL

Consider a connected undirected graph $G = (V, E)$ with no self-loops. Let D (for "destination") be a distinguished vertex in V. We denote the neighbors of vertex v in G by $N_G(v)$. A directed graph $\vec{G} = (V, \vec{E})$ is an *orientation* of G if for each (u, v) in $\vec{E}$, $\{u, v\}$ is in E, and for each $\{u, v\}$ in E, exactly one of (u, v) and (v, u) is in $\vec{E}$. A vertex v in V is a *sink* in $\vec{G}$ if it has no outgoing links, i.e., there is no link (v, u) in $\vec{E}$ for any u. A *chain* in $\vec{G}$ is a sequence of vertices, $\langle v_1, v_2, \ldots, v_k \rangle$, such that for each i, $1 \le i < k$, either (v_i, v_{i+1}) or (v_{i+1}, v_i) is in $\vec{E}$. Each (v_i, v_{i+1}) is said to be a *link* in the chain; if (v_{i+1}, v_i) is in $\vec{E}$, then the link is said to be *wrong-way* in the chain, otherwise it is *right-way*. If $k = 1$, then the chain consists of a single vertex (and no links). A chain is a *path* if it has no wrong-way links. A *circuit* is a chain in which $v_k = v_1$. A *cycle* is a circuit with no wrong-way links. $\vec{G}$ is said to be *destination-oriented*, or *D-oriented*, if there is a path from each vertex to D.

The problem to be solved is the following:

- Given an orientation of a graph $G = (V, E)$ with distinguished vertex D, change the direction of some subset of E so that the resulting orientation of G is D-oriented.

See Figure 2.1 for an example. Throughout, we indicate sink nodes as shaded circles and the destination with two concentric circles in the figures.

The original application for this problem, as discussed by Gafni and Bertsekas [19], is routing messages in a network of computing nodes. D corresponds to the destination node of the messages and the directions of the links tell the nodes in which directions to forward messages for that destination. Furthermore, if the graph is acyclic, then the routes will be loop-free.

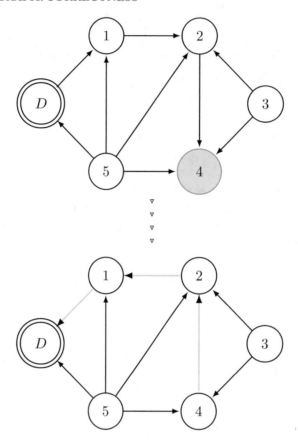

Figure 2.1: The upper graph is not destination-oriented, and in fact, vertex 4 is a sink. However, by reversing the links $(D, 1)$, $(1, 2)$, and $(2, 4)$, as indicated by the light grey links in the bottom graph, a destination-oriented graph is obtained.

Looking forward toward distributed solutions to the problem, we would prefer "local" approaches in which computing nodes associated with graph vertices could decide based only on local information which incident links, if any, should be reversed. The property of being a sink can be determined locally, and this is the starting point for developing algorithms to solve the problem.

First, we review some basic facts about acyclic graphs.

Lemma 2.1   *If $\vec{G}$ is acyclic, then every vertex in V has a path to some sink.*

Proof. Suppose in contradiction, that some vertex v in V has no path to a sink, possibly because there is no sink in $\vec{G}$. Let S be the (possibly empty) set of sinks in $\vec{G}$. We inductively construct an infinite path $v_0, v_1, \ldots$ in $\vec{G}$. Let v_0 be v. For each $i > 0$, let v_i be any vertex in V such that $(v_{i-1}, v_i) \in \vec{E}$; v_i exists by the assumption that there is no path from v to any sink. Since V is finite, there must exist i and j, $i < j$, such that $v_i = v_j$, which means that there is a cycle in $\vec{G}$, a contradiction. ∎

Lemma 2.1 implies that if $\vec{G}$ is acyclic, then it has at least one sink.

Lemma 2.2   *Let $\vec{G}$ be acyclic. Then $\vec{G}$ is D-oriented if and only if D is the unique sink in $\vec{G}$.*

Proof.   Suppose $\vec{G}$ is D-oriented. By definition, every vertex has a path to D, and thus every vertex other than D is not a sink. By Lemma 2.1, some vertex in $\vec{G}$ must be a sink, implying D is the unique sink.

Suppose D is the unique sink in $\vec{G}$. Then by Lemma 2.1, every vertex in V has a path to D, and thus $\vec{G}$ is D-oriented. ∎

We consider a generic approach to this problem, which consists of repeatedly reversing some of the links incident on some of the sink vertices. In more detail, the *Generic Link Reversal (GLR) algorithm* operates as follows (see Algorithm 1 for the pseudocode): Start with an initial directed graph. At each iteration, choose some nonempty subset S of the sink vertices. The set S cannot include D, even if D happens to be a sink. Then reverse some of the links incident on these vertices. The vertices in S are said to "take a step" at this iteration. Allowing more than one sink to take a step at the same iteration provides more concurrency.

Algorithm 1: Generic Link Reversal (GLR)

Input: directed graph $\vec{G} = (V, \vec{E})$ with distinguished $D \in V$
1 **while** $\vec{G}$ has a sink other than D **do**
2 | choose a nonempty subset S of sinks in $\vec{G}$, not including D
3 | reverse the direction of a nonempty subset of the links incident on vertices in S
4 **end**

By the termination condition of the while loop, if the algorithm finishes, the result has no sink other than possibly D. By Lemma 2.2, if the final graph is acyclic, then it is also D-oriented. The first question is how to choose the sinks S and the incident links to reverse in a way that ensures termination. Not all choices will lead to termination: for instance, consider a chain

$$D \rightarrow x \leftarrow y$$

and suppose that x reverses its right link, then y reverses its left link, then x reverses its right link, etc. forever. The second question is how to make the choices so that, if the graph is acyclic initially, it remains acyclic, so as to ensure D-orientation at the end. Different methods for deciding which links to reverse give rise to different "link reversal" algorithms.

Two algorithms were proposed by Gafni and Bertsekas [19] which address these questions. In the first algorithm, the *Full Reversal (FR) algorithm*, S can be any nonempty subset of the sinks, excluding D, and all links incident upon vertices in S are reversed. See Algorithm 2 for the pseudocode and Figure 2.2 for an example execution of FR.

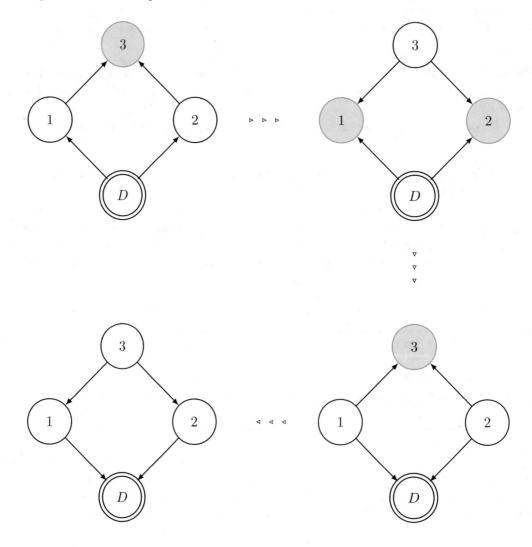

Figure 2.2: Example execution of FR.

Algorithm 2: Full Reversal (FR)

Input: directed graph $\vec{G} = (V, \vec{E})$ with distinguished $D \in V$
1 **while** $\vec{G}$ has a sink other than D **do**
2   choose a nonempty subset S of sinks in $\vec{G}$, not including D
3   **foreach** $v \in S$ **do** reverse the direction of all links incident on v
4 **end**

Lemma 2.3 *FR terminates.*

Proof. Suppose in contradiction that there is some execution of FR that does not terminate. Let W be the set of all vertices that are chosen infinitely often to be part of S in Line 2. Since V is finite, W is nonempty. Note that $V - W$ is nonempty as it contains at least D. Since G is connected, there is an edge $\{u, v\}$ in E where $u \in W$ and $v \in V - W$. Let t be the iteration of the while loop at which v takes its last step; if v takes no steps at all, let $t = 0$. When u takes its next step after iteration t, the link (v, u) is reversed to be directed from u to v. But since v takes no more steps after iteration t, the link remains directed away from u. Thus, u never becomes a sink again and takes no more steps, contradiction. ∎

Lemma 2.4 *FR maintains acyclicity.*

Proof. We show that each iteration of FR maintains acyclicity. Suppose in contradiction there is an iteration such that the graph is acyclic before the reversals but has a cycle afterwards. Let S be the set of sinks whose incident links are reversed in this iteration. The newly created cycle must include some vertex $v \in S$, since only links incident on vertices in S were reversed. But v has no incoming links after the reversal and thus cannot be part of a cycle. ∎

The previous lemmas give us:

Theorem 2.5 If the input graph to FR is acyclic, then the output is acyclic and destination-oriented.

Proof. Lemma 2.3 states that the execution terminates, so there is a final graph in which no vertex, except possibly D, is a sink. Suppose the input graph is acyclic. Then Lemma 2.4 implies that the final graph is acyclic. By Lemma 2.1, D is a sink in the final graph, and so by Lemma 2.2, the final graph is D-oriented. ∎

In some executions of FR on some initial graphs, some links can repeatedly reverse (cf. the edge between vertices 2 and 3 in Figure 2.2). Possibly in an attempt to reduce the number of link reversals, Gafni and Bertsekas [19] proposed another link reversal algorithm, called *Partial Reversal (PR)*. Roughly speaking, in PR, the set of links to be reversed is computed as follows for each sink v in the chosen set of sinks S: A link (u, v) is reversed by v if and only if the link has not been reversed by u since the last iteration in which v took a step.

Algorithm 3 is the pseudocode for PR. For each vertex u other than D, the variable $list[u]$ keeps track of which neighbors of u have reversed the shared link since the last time u took a step. Whenever neighbor v of u reverses the shared link, v is added to $list[u]$ (Line 9), and whenever u takes a step, $list[u]$ is emptied (Line 10). When v takes a step, it reverses each incident link whose other endpoint is not in $list[v]$ (Lines 5-6). However, if all v's neighbors are in $list[v]$, then v reverses all its incident links (Lines 7-8). These rules ensure that v reverses at least one link at each step, no matter what the contents of $list[v]$ are. See Figure 2.3 for an example execution of PR.

Algorithm 3: Partial Reversal (PR)

Input: directed graph $\vec{G} = (V, \vec{E})$ with distinguished $D \in V$

1 **foreach** $v \in V$ **do** $list[v] := \emptyset$

2 **while** $\vec{G}$ has a sink other than D **do**

3   choose a nonempty subset S of sinks in $\vec{G}$, not including D

4   **foreach** $v \in S$ **do**

5   **if** $N_G(v) \neq list[v]$ **then**

6   reverse the direction of all links incident on v whose source is not in $list[v]$

7   **else**   // all neighbors of v are in list[v]

8   reverse the direction of all links incident on v

9   **end**

10   **foreach** u such that (u, v) was just reversed **do** add v to $list[u]$

11          $list[v] := \emptyset$

12   **end**

13 **end**

Lemma 2.6   *PR terminates.*

Proof. Suppose in contradiction that there is some execution of PR that does not terminate. Let W be the set of all vertices that are chosen infinitely often to be part of S in Line 2. Since V is finite, W is nonempty. Note that $V - W$ is nonempty as it contains at least D. Since G is connected, there is an edge $\{u, v\}$ in E where $u \in W$ and $v \in V - W$. Let t be the iteration of the while loop at which v takes its last step; if v takes no steps, let $t = 0$.

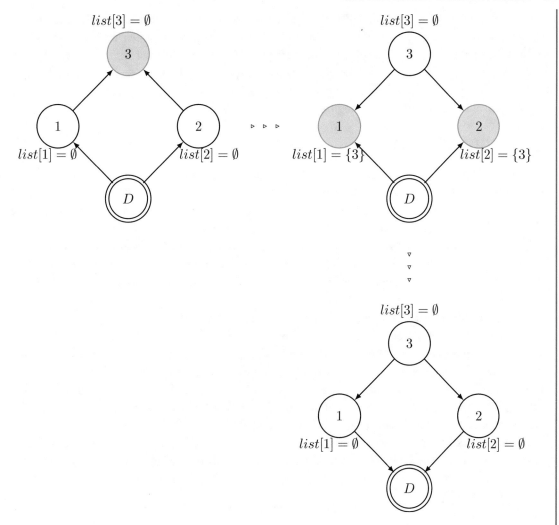

Figure 2.3: Example execution of PR.

We now show that vertex u reverses (v, u) in either its first or second step after iteration t. Suppose u does not reverse (v, u) in its first step after iteration t. At the end of this step, $list[u]$ is emptied. Since v takes no more steps, v is never subsequently added to $list[u]$. Then when u takes its second step after iteration t, v is not in $list[u]$ and so the link (v, u) is reversed to be directed from u to v.

Thus, after at most the second step by u after iteration t, the edge $\{u, v\}$ remains directed away from u. Since u never again becomes a sink, it takes no more steps, a contradiction. ∎

We would like to show that PR, like FR, preserves acyclicity, and thus ensures destination-orientation on initial graphs that are acyclic. However, a direct proof is rather involved, and so we defer a discussion of the acyclicity of PR until Section 2.3 (see discussion just before Corollary 2.19).

We next consider two different approaches to instantiating the Generic Link Reversal algorithm, one based on vertex labels and one based on link labels. Both approaches encompass FR and PR as special cases, as well as allowing the possibility of other schemes.

2.2   VERTEX LABELS

Gafni and Bertsekas [19] proposed using vertex labels, or *heights*, to implement GLR. The labels are chosen from a totally ordered set. The vertex labels are used to induce an orientation $\vec{G}$ of undirected graph G as follows: the link between vertices u and v in $\vec{G}$ is directed from u to v if and only if the label of u is greater than the label of v. Thus, a sink corresponds to a vertex whose height is a local minimum. In order to reverse the direction of the link from u to v, v increases its label to be more than the label of u. This approach requires that vertices know the labels of their neighbors (as well as their own). For now, assume that they have access to this information instantaneously; in Section 4 we discuss how to relax this assumption.

In more detail, let L be a totally ordered, countably infinite set of *labels* that is partitioned into a collection $\{L_v : v \in V\}$ of disjoint subsets. The subset L_v is used by vertex v; since the subsets are disjoint, no two vertices ever have the same label and thus the direction of each edge is always well-defined. We require each L_v to be countably infinite and unbounded[1]. Let $\mathcal{L}$ be the set of all functions h from V to L such that $h(v) \in L_v$ for all $v \in V$. Each function h in $\mathcal{L}$ is called a *vertex labeling* of graph G; h induces an orientation of G, denoted $h.G$, which is defined to be $(V, \vec{E})$, where (u, v) is in $\vec{E}$ if and only if $\{u, v\}$ is in E and $h(u) > h(v)$.

For each vertex $v \in V$, we define a function g_v from vertex labelings of G to labels for vertex v that produces a new label for v. The function must depend only on the labels of v and the neighbors of v, and it must be increasing. In more detail, g_v is a function from $\mathcal{L}$ to L_v such that

- if $h(u) = h'(u)$ for all $u \in \{v\} \cup N_G(v)$, then $g_v(h) = g_v(h')$; and

- for every infinite sequence $\langle h_1, h_2, \ldots \rangle$ of vertex labelings of G such that v is a sink in $h_i.G$ and $h_{i+1}(v) = g_v(h_i)$ for all $i \geq 1$, the sequence $\langle h_1(v), h_2(v), \ldots \rangle$ increases without bound.

The first item above says that if two vertex labelings h and h' agree on the labels for a node v and all v's neighbors, then v's labeling function g_v produces the same new label for v when it is applied to h as when it is applied to h'.

The second item above says that in any infinite sequence of vertex labelings in which v is a sink in every labeling, and in which the label of v in each labeling is the result of applying v's labeling function to the previous labeling, the sequence of labels taken on by v must increase without bound, regardless of what changes might take place in the labels of v's neighbors.

---

[1]*Unbounded* means there is no element a^* in L and no v such that for all $a \in L_v$, $a < a^*$ in the total order.

Given a collection of such functions g_v, the Increasing Vertex Labels (IVL) pseudocode appears in Algorithm 4.

Algorithm 4: Increasing Vertex Labels (IVL)

Input: undirected graph $G = (V, E)$ with distinguished $D \in V$ and vertex labeling h

1 **while** $h.G$ has a sink other than D **do**

2   choose a nonempty subset S of sinks in $h.G$, not including D

3   **foreach** $v \in S$ **do** $h(v) := g_v(h)$

4 **end**

Lemma 2.7   *IVL terminates.*

Proof.   Assume in contradiction that there is an execution of IVL that does not terminate. Let W be the set of all vertices that are chosen infinitely often to be part of S in Line 2; these are the vertices that perform an infinite number of reversals. Since V is finite, W is nonempty. Note that $V - W$ is nonempty as it contains at least D. Since G is connected, there is an edge $\{u, v\}$ in E with $u \in W$ and $v \in V - W$. Let t be the iteration of the while loop at which v takes its last step; if v takes no steps, let $t = 0$. After t, the label of v does not change. However, the label of u increases every time u takes a step after t. Since u takes infinitely many steps and its label increases without bound, eventually its label exceeds the final label of v and the edge is directed from u to v. Since v takes no more steps, the edge remains directed from u to v and u takes no more steps, contradiction. ∎

Lemma 2.8   *IVL maintains acyclicity.*

Proof.   The orientation of G at each iteration is induced by the vertex labels. Since the vertex labels are drawn from a totally ordered set and two vertices never have the same label, $h.G$ is always acyclic. ∎

The previous two lemmas and Lemma 2.2 imply:

Theorem 2.9   IVL ensures destination-orientation.

Gafni and Bertsekas [19] also prove that, starting from the same initial graph, no matter which subset of sinks takes steps at each iteration of IVL and no matter in which order, the final destination-oriented graph is the same. And in fact, each vertex experiences the same number of reversals.

The *Pair Algorithm* was proposed by Gafni and Bertsekas [19] as a means of implementing the FR algorithm by instantiating IVL. For simplicity, we assume that $V = \{0, 1, \ldots, n\}$, with vertex

0 being the destination. Each label for vertex $v \in V$ is an ordered pair of integers (c, v). A sink changes its label by setting the first component to be one larger than the largest first component in the labels of all its neighbors.

In the terminology of the IVL algorithm, for each $v \in V$, $L_v = \mathbb{N} \times \{v\}$. Labels are compared using lexicographic ordering. For each $v \in V$, g_v is defined as follows: $g_v(h) = (1 + \max(C), v)$, where $C = \{c : h(u) = (c, u)$ for some $u \in N_G(v)\}$.

Lemma 2.10   *The Pair algorithm is a special case of the IVL algorithm.*

Proof.   By definition, each L_v is countably infinite, totally ordered, and unbounded with respect to the lexicographic ordering. Observe that each g_v depends only on the labels of the neighbors of v, and that repeated application of g_v results in labels that increase without bound.   ∎

The *Triple Algorithm* was proposed by Gafni and Bertsekas [19] as a way of implementing the PR algorithm, although this correspondence was not proved. Each label for vertex $v \in V$ is an ordered triple of integers (a, b, v). The label of a sink vertex v is changed to ensure that the new label is larger than those of neighbors with the smallest first component among all of v's neighbors, but smaller than the labels of all other neighbors.

In the terminology of the IVL algorithm, for each $v \in V$, $L_v = \mathbb{N} \times \mathbb{Z} \times \{v\}$. Labels are compared using lexicographic ordering. For each $v \in V$, $g_v(h)$ is defined to be (a_1, b_1, v), where a_1 and b_1 are computed as follows. Let $h(v) = (a_0, b_0, v)$.

- Define a_1 to be $\min(A) + 1$, where $A = \{a : h(u) = (a, b, u)$ for some $u \in N_G(v)$ and some $b\}$.

- Let $B = \{b : h(u) = (a_1, b, u)$ for some $u \in N_G(v)\}$. If $B = \emptyset$, then define b_1 to be b_0, otherwise define b_1 to be $\min(B) - 1$.

Lemma 2.11   *The Triple algorithm is a special case of the IVL algorithm.*

Proof.   By definition, each L_v is countably infinite and totally ordered and unbounded with respect to the lexicographic ordering. Observe that each g_v depends only on the labels of v and the neighbors of v, and that repeated application of g_v results in labels that increase without bound.   ∎

As a result of the three previous lemmas and Lemma 2.7, we have:

Corollary 2.12   *The Pair and Triple algorithms both terminate with a destination-oriented graph.*

As an alternative argument for the termination of the Pair algorithm, we observe that the Pair algorithm corresponds to FR, which has an easy termination proof. The situation is not so easy for the Triple algorithm, since the correspondence with PR is not so straightforward. Such a correspondence would also show that acyclicity is preserved by PR.

2.3   LINK LABELS

Let's take an alternative look at how to implement link reversal algorithms. Instead of labeling vertices, we label links, and instead of using unbounded labels, we use binary labels. This approach was suggested by Charron-Bost et al. [11].

Consider an orientation $\vec{G} = (V, \vec{E})$ of a connected undirected graph $G = (V, E)$ with no self loops and a distinguished vertex D. Let l be a *binary link labeling* of $\vec{G}$, i.e., a function from $\vec{E}$ to $\{0, 1\}$. Denote by $\vec{G}^l$ the graph $\vec{G}$ with its edges labeled by l. A link in $\vec{G}^l$ is said to be *marked* if it is labeled with 1, otherwise it is *unmarked*. The labels can be interpreted as some history information and determine which links are reversed by a sink.

The Binary Link Labels (BLL) algorithm works as follows (see Algorithm 5 for pseudocode). Suppose v is a sink vertex chosen at some iteration. One of the following two rules is applied to v's incident links.

- LR1: If at least one incident link is labeled with 0, then reverse all the incident links labeled with 0 and flip the labels on *all* incident links.

- LR2: If no incident link is labeled with 0, then reverse all the incident links.

Note that in rule LR2, no labels are changed. Ignoring the initial state, if a link (u, v) is labeled with 1, it indicates that this link was reversed during the most recent previous step by u. The next time that v takes a step, say at iteration t, the link is not reversed but the label is changed to 0. The next time after iteration t that v takes a step, the link is reversed to become (v, u) and the label changed to 1. Thus for each incoming link on a vertex, after either one or two reversals by the vertex, the link becomes outgoing.

Algorithm 5: Binary Link Labels (BLL)

Input: directed graph $\vec{G} = (V, \vec{E})$ with distinguished $D \in V$, and binary link labeling l of $\vec{G}$

1 **while** $\vec{G}$ has a sink other than D **do**
2   choose a nonempty subset S of sinks in $\vec{G}$, not including D
3   **foreach** $v \in S$ **do**
4   **if** v has an unmarked incident link **then**   // (LR1)
5   reverse the direction of all v's unmarked incident links
6   flip the label on all v's incident links
7   **else**   // v has no unmarked incident link (LR2)
8   reverse the direction of all v's incident links
9   **end**
10   **end**
11 **end**

The next Lemma shows that no matter how the links are labeled, BLL always terminates.

Lemma 2.13   *BLL terminates.*

Proof.   Assume in contradiction that there is some execution of BLL that does not terminate. Let W be the set of all vertices that are chosen infinitely often to be part of S in Line 2; these are the vertices that perform an infinite number of reversals. Since V is finite, W is nonempty. Note that $V - W$ is nonempty as it contains at least D. Since G is connected, there is an edge $\{u, v\}$ in E where $u \in W$ and $v \in V - W$. Let t be the iteration of the while loop at which v takes its last step; if v takes no steps, let $t = 0$. After t, the label of v does not change.

We now show that vertex u reverses (v, u) in either its first or second step after iteration t. Suppose u does not reverse (v, u) in its first step after iteration t. Since this link was not reversed, it must have been marked (labeled with 1), and as a result of the LR1 step, its label is changed to 0. Then when u takes its second step after iteration t, the link (v, u) which is now labeled with 0, is reversed to be directed from u to v.

Thus, after at most the second step by u after iteration t, the edge $\{u, v\}$ remains directed away from u. Since u never again becomes a sink, it takes no more steps, contradiction. ∎

Even if the input graph is acyclic, BLL does not maintain acyclicity for every link labeling of the input graph; see Figure 2.4 for an example. However, there is a sufficient condition on the link labeling that ensures that acyclicity is maintained, which we present next.

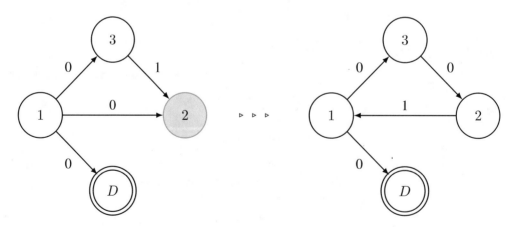

Figure 2.4: An execution in which BLL does not preserve acyclicity.

Let $\chi = \langle v_1, v_2, \ldots, v_k \rangle$ be a chain in $\vec{G}^l$. We define the following quantities with respect to χ:

- Let r be the number of *marked* links in χ that are right-way, i.e., the number of indices i such that (v_i, v_{i+1}) is in $\vec{E}$.

- Let w be the number of *marked* links in χ that are wrong-way.

- Index i, $1 \le i \le k$, is said to be an *occurrence* of a vertex v in χ if $v_i = v$; if $v_1 = v_k$, then this is considered only a single occurrence of v. Let s be the number of occurrences of vertices such that the two links of χ adjacent to the occurrence are both incoming to the vertex and are both *unmarked*.

For example, in the graph shown in Figure 2.5, consider circuit $\langle 1, 2, \ldots, 8, 1 \rangle$: vertex 3 has both incoming links unmarked, so $s = 1$; links $(1, 2)$ and $(4, 5)$ are right-way and marked, so $r = 2$; and link $(7, 6)$ is wrong-way and marked, so $w = 1$.

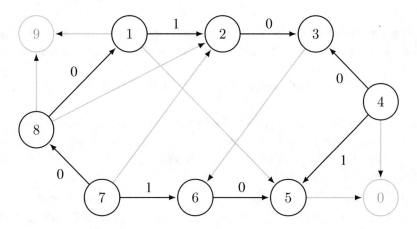

Figure 2.5: Example graph for circuit concepts.

Lemma 2.14   *For any circuit χ in $\vec{G}^l$, if $(w + s) \cdot (r + s) > 0$, then χ is not a cycle.*

Proof.   By definition, the product cannot be negative. Suppose χ is a cycle. By definition of a cycle, no links are wrong-way, so $w = 0$. Also, $s = 0$, since no vertex is a sink with respect to χ. Thus, the product is 0. ∎

We say that $\vec{G}^l$ *satisfies the Acyclicity Property (AC)* if, for every circuit in $\vec{G}^l$,

$$(w + s)(r + s) > 0.$$

Charron-Bost et al. [11] proved that the quantities $(w + s)$ and $(r + s)$ for a given circuit never change throughout the execution of BLL. The proof is by a case analysis that considers, for each vertex that takes a step, which rule (LR1 or LR2) is executed and what the relevant link labels are. The key observation is that changes to w and r are cancelled out by changes to s. Thus, we have:

Lemma 2.15   *If the input graph $\vec{G}$ is acyclic and the input link labeling l is such that $\vec{G}^l$ satisfies property AC, then BLL maintains acyclicity.*

Thus, we have:

Theorem 2.16   If the input graph $\vec{G}$ is acyclic and the input link labeling l is such that $\vec{G}^l$ satisfies property AC, then BLL outputs an acyclic destination-oriented graph.

We next argue that FR and PR are special cases of BLL.

Lemma 2.17   *If all links of $\vec{G}$ are initially labeled with 1, then BLL equals FR.*

Proof.   A simple induction on the iterations of the while loop shows that since all links are always labeled 1, only the LR2 rule is executed, and thus all links incident on a sink are always reversed.   ∎

Lemma 2.18   *If all links of $\vec{G}$ are initially labeled with 0, then BLL equals PR.*

Proof.   The first step by a vertex v reverses all of v's incident links and labels them with 1. Thus, label 1 on link (v, u) means the link was reversed since the last time u was a sink. After the next reversal by u, the link remains incoming but the label is changed to 0. Thus, label 0 means that the link should be reversed the next time u takes a step.   ∎

Suppose $\vec{G}$ is acyclic. Then $\vec{G}$ satisfies AC under the all-1's labeling (FR), since for every circuit, w and r are both positive. Also, $\vec{G}$ satisfies AC under the all-0's labeling (PR), since for every circuit, s is positive. Thus, we have the following corollary, which is an alternate proof of Theorem 2.5, and answers affirmatively the question raised earlier whether PR preserves acyclicity.

Corollary 2.19   *If the input graph $\vec{G}$ is acyclic, then FR and PR both output an acyclic destination-oriented graph.*

Radeva and Lynch [37] gave a direct proof that PR preserves acyclicity; the graph is viewed as embedded in the plane and the proof employs geometric arguments.

BLL can be instantiated in ways other than FR and PR, by initializing the link labels differently. Section 3.1.3 looks at what benefits, if any, might accrue from other initializations.

We close this subsection with a short comparison of IVL and BLL. An advantage of the binary link labeling approach over the increasing vertex labeling approach is the limited space required by the former. However, BLL relies on the input already being a directed graph (perhaps even acyclic), whereas with IVL, the algorithm imposes the initial directions via the vertex labels, and cycles simply cannot arise. There is thus a tradeoff between space usage and the effort required to ensure directed links.

CHAPTER 3

Routing in a Graph: Complexity

In this section we study the work and time complexity of the routing algorithms from the previous section. Section 3.1 covers work complexity; it first gives the results that were obtained for the vertex-labeling algorithms, then presents the results for the link-labeling algorithms, and concludes with a game-theoretic comparison of FR and PR. Time complexity results are presented in Section 3.2, primarily for the link-labeling algorithms; first, FR is dealt with and then a transformation is sketched that gives the time complexity for PR.

3.1 WORK COMPLEXITY

Busch et al. [4, 5] initiated a systematic study of the complexity of link reversal algorithms. Given an execution of any of the specializations of the Generic Link Reversal algorithm presented so far, let the *work complexity* of vertex v be the number of reversals done by v, and denote this quantity by σ_v. As noted by Gafni and Bertsekas [19] for IVL, the work complexity of a vertex is the same in all executions; the same is true for BLL, and for the same reason, which is that two neighboring vertices cannot be sinks simultaneously. The *global work complexity*, denoted σ, is the sum of the work complexities of all the vertices.

A vertex is called *bad* if it has no path to the destination, otherwise it is called *good*. It can be shown by induction on the distance from the destination that good vertices never take steps.

3.1.1 VERTEX LABELING

Here we give a short overview of the results in [4, 5], regarding the work complexity of the Pair and Triple algorithms as well as the work complexity of a generalization of those algorithms.

Pair Algorithm. Let h be any Pair algorithm vertex labeling for input graph G. Given the resulting orientation $h.G$, partition V into layers recursively as follows. Let L_0 be the set of all good vertices. For $k > 0$, vertex v is in layer L_k if k is the smallest integer such that one of the following is true: there is an incoming link to v from a vertex in layer L_{k-1}, or there is an outgoing link from v to a vertex in layer L_k.

It is shown in [4, 5] that each vertex that is initially in layer L_j takes *exactly* j steps. Thus, $\sigma_v = j$, where $v \in L_j$.

If there are n_b bad vertices in $h.G$, then, since the maximum layer index is n_b, the global work complexity is $O(n_b^2)$. In fact, this bound is tight, in the sense that, for every $n_b > 0$, there is a graph with n_b bad vertices in which the global work complexity of the Pair algorithm is $\Omega(n_b^2)$.

Triple Algorithm.   Let h be any Triple algorithm vertex labeling for input graph G. Call the first component of a triple the *alpha value*. Let a^{max} be the largest alpha value and a^{min} be the smallest alpha value in orientation $h.G$. Busch et al. [4, 5] showed that the alpha value of a vertex v at distance d in G from a good vertex never exceeds $a^{max} + d$. Since the initial alpha value of v is at least a^{min} and each reversal by v increases its alpha value by at least 1, the number of reversals done by v is *at most $a^{max} - a^{min} + d$*. If the Triple algorithm is initialized so that all the alpha values are 0, then $\sigma_v \leq d$.

To bound the global work complexity when there are n_b bad vertices, note that d is at most n_b, so the total number of reversals is *at most $a^* n_b + n_b^2$*, where $a^* = a^{max} - a^{min}$. If the Triple algorithm is initialized so that all the alpha values are 0, then $\sigma = O(n_b^2)$.

These bounds are shown to be *asymptotically* tight for a certain class of input graphs. (It can be shown that the gap between the upper and lower bounds in [4, 5] for a vertex is at most a factor of 8 [20].) For any graph in the class, the vertices are partitioned into an indexed sequence of subsets and the work complexity of each vertex is proved to be at least half the index of the subset to which the vertex belongs. A graph in this class is constructed with n_b bad vertices and $\Omega(n_b^2)$ global work complexity.

Perhaps counter-intuitively, the worst-case work complexity for the Triple Algorithm is at least as bad as that of the Pair algorithm. In fact, it can be arbitrarily worse, if the triples are initialized adversarially to have a large discrepancy between the largest and smallest alpha value.

IVL.   Busch et al. [4, 5] also showed a more general lower bound on work complexity. For the Increasing Vertex Labels algorithm, the worst-case global work complexity is $\Omega(n_b^2)$, where n_b is the number of bad vertices in the labeled input graph. Similarly to the case for the Pair and Triple algorithms, a family of specific graphs is described with the expensive behavior.

3.1.2   LINK LABELING

Charron-Bost et al. [11] developed an exact formula for the work complexity of BLL. The formula holds for every vertex in every input graph satisfying AC. By specializing the general formula for the all-1's initial labeling, an exact work complexity analysis for FR is obtained, which is an alternative to the analysis discussed in Section 3.1.1 for the Pair algorithm. By specializing the general formula for the all-0's initial labeling, an exact work complexity analysis for PR is obtained. This result is a tightening and expansion of the analysis discussed in Section 3.1.1 for the Triple algorithm when all alpha values are initially 0.

Let l be any binary link-labeling of input graph $\vec{G} = (V, \vec{E})$ (which is an orientation of a connected undirected graph $G = (V, E)$ with no self-loops and a distinguished vertex D) such that $\vec{G}^l$ satisfies AC. We now analyze the work complexity of BLL, following Charron-Bost et al. [11].

Let $\chi = \langle v_1, v_2, \ldots, v_k \rangle$ be any chain in $\vec{G}^l$. Recall the definitions of r and s for χ given just before Lemma 2.14: r is the number of marked links that are right-way and s is the number of occurrences of vertices such that the two links adjacent to the occurrence are both incoming and unmarked. We make the following additional definitions with respect to χ:

- Let *Res* equal 1 if the *last* link in χ is *unmarked* and right-way (i.e., (v_{k-1}, v_k) is in $\vec{E}$), and 0 otherwise.

- Let ω be $2(r + s) + Res$.

For example, consider vertex 5 in the directed graph in Figure 3.1. For chain $\langle D, 7, 6, 5 \rangle$: $r = 1, s = 0, Res = 1$, and $\omega = 3$. For chain $\langle D, 1, 2, 3, 4, 5 \rangle$: $r = 2, s = 1, Res = 0$, and $\omega = 6$.

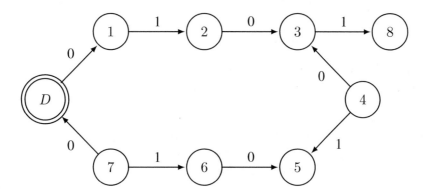

Figure 3.1: Example graph for chain concepts.

We show in Lemma 3.1 below that a reversal done by v decreases the ω value of all chains from D to v by the same amount and that reversals done by other vertices have no effect on the ω values of the chains from D to v[1].

By Theorem 2.16, when the algorithm terminates, at least one chain from D to v has the property that its reverse is a *path* from v to D. The value of ω for that chain is 0 since there are no right-way links in the chain, i.e., all links are directed toward D. Once at least one chain from v to D has this property, v takes no more steps, as it is now good. (In fact, v stops doing reversals as soon as ω is 0 for some chain, which might be before the property is true. For example, suppose all the links in the graph shown in Figure 2.3 are initially labeled with 0 and then BLL is executed. After the first step by vertex 3, both chains from D to 3 have ω equal to 0 although there is not yet a path from 3 to D.) Thus, the number of reversals by v is the number required for the reverse of a D-to-v chain to become a path for the first time. That is, the number of reversals made by v is a function of the following quantity:

- Let ω_{min} be the minimum, over all chains χ from D to v, of ω for χ.

To calculate the number of reversals, we must quantify the amount by which ω_{min} decreases when v takes a step. The amount depends on the classification of v into one of three disjoint

---

[1] For consistency with the material on time complexity of BLL presented later in Section 3.2, here we consider chains between a vertex v and the destination D to start with D and end with v, instead of the reverse as is done in [11].

categories. The specific function of ω_{min} depends on the initial classification of the vertex into one of the three categories and the manner in which vertices migrate between the categories. Lemma 3.2 identifies how vertices migrate between categories and Theorem 3.3 puts all the pieces together.

Details follow. Partition $V \setminus \{D\}$ into three categories:

- $\mathcal{S}$ consists of all $v \in V \setminus \{D\}$ such that all of v's incident links are incoming and unmarked (i.e., v is a sink with all its links labeled 0).

- $\mathcal{N}$ consists of all $v \in V \setminus \{D\}$ such that v has no unmarked incoming links (i.e., all of v's incoming links, if any, are labeled 1).

- $\mathcal{O}$ consists of all other $v \in V \setminus \{D\}$ (i.e., either v is a sink with a mix of marked and unmarked incident links, or v is not a sink and has an unmarked incoming link).

Lemma 3.1   *Let χ be a chain from D to v in $\vec{G}^l$ and consider ω for χ. Suppose some vertex u takes a step. Suppose $u = v$. Then if $v \in \mathcal{S}$, then ω decreases by 1; if $v \in \mathcal{N}$, then ω decreases by 2; and if $v \in \mathcal{O}$, then ω decreases by 1. If $u \neq v$, then ω does not change.*

Proof.   Suppose $v \in \mathcal{S}$ takes a step. Since v is in $\mathcal{S}$, all its incident links are unmarked and rule (LR1) is executed. The only change to the links of the chain is that the last link goes from unmarked and incoming at v to marked and outgoing at v. Since the last link is no longer unmarked and incoming, *Res* goes from 1 to 0. The change does not affect the number of marked links that are right-way in the chain, so r is unchanged. The only way that s could be affected is if the neighbor of v in the chain now has both its incident links in the chain incoming and unmarked; but the link between v and its neighbor becomes marked, and thus s does not change. Finally, since $\omega = 2(r + s) + Res$, it follows that ω decreases by 1.

Suppose $v \in \mathcal{N}$ takes a step. Since v is in $\mathcal{N}$, all its incident links are marked and rule (LR2) is executed. The last link in the chain goes from marked and incoming at v to marked and outgoing at v. Thus, r decreases by 1 and ω decreases by 2.

Suppose $v \in \mathcal{O}$ takes a step. Since v is in $\mathcal{O}$, at least one incident link is marked and at least one is unmarked, and rule (LR1) is executed. If the link that is part of χ is unmarked, then *Res* goes from 1 to 0, and ω decreases by 1. If the link that is part of χ is marked, then r decreases by 1, *Res* goes from 0 to 1, and ω decreases by 1.

If u is not a part of χ, then none of the links in χ change and neither does ω. Suppose u is part of χ. By considering every case (whether rule (LR1) or (LR2) is executed and the labels of the links in χ that are incident on u), we can verify that ω is unchanged. As one example, consider the situation when both links in χ that are incident on u are labeled 0 and some other link incident on u is labeled 1. Then rule (LR1) is executed, which causes the two links in χ that are incident on u to reverse direction and become labeled with 1. As a result, r increases by 1 but s decreases by 1, leaving ω unchanged, since *Res* is also unchanged.   ∎

Lemma 3.2   *Choose any vertex $v \in V$ and suppose that some vertex $u \in V$ takes a step. Suppose $u = v$. Then if $v \in S$, then v moves to N; if $v \in N$, then v does not change category; and if $v \in O$, then v does not change category. If $u \neq v$, then v does not change category.*

Proof.   Suppose $u = v$. If v is in S, rule (LR1) is executed and all of v's incident links are made outgoing and marked. Thus, v is now in N.

If v is in N, rule (LR2) is executed and all of v's incident links are made outgoing and remain marked. Thus, v is still in N.

If v is in O, rule (LR1) is executed. As a result, all of v's unmarked incoming links become outgoing and marked, whereas all of v's marked incoming links remain incoming but become unmarked. Thus, v is still in O.

Suppose $u \neq v$. A reversal by a vertex other than one of v's neighbors does not affect any links incident on v and thus v's category is unaffected. Suppose u is a neighbor of v. Since u is a sink, v cannot be a sink and thus v is not in S. A case analysis can be done to verify that the reversal done by u does not change the classification of v. As an example, consider the case when v is in O and the link from v to u is unmarked. By definition of O, v has another incident link that is incoming and unmarked. After u takes a step, the link between v and u is directed toward u and is marked, while the other link incident on v is still incoming and unmarked. If v is now a sink, it has a mix of marked and unmarked incoming links, and even if it is not a sink, it still has an unmarked incoming link. Thus, v remains in O. ∎

Theorem 3.3   Consider any execution of BLL on input graph $\vec{G}$ and binary link labeling l such that $\vec{G}^l$ satisfies AC. Let v be any vertex in V.

- If $v \in S$ initially, then the number of reversals done by v is $(\omega_{min} + 1)/2$.

- If $v \in N$ initially, then the number of reversals done by v is $\omega_{min}/2$.

- If $v \in O$ initially, then the number of reversals done by v is ω_{min}.

Proof.   If v is initially in S, then after v's first reversal, ω_{min} decreases by 1 and v is in N. Once v is in N, it stays there, and every subsequent reversal by v decreases ω_{min} by 2. If v is initially in O, then v is always in O and every reversal by v reduces ω_{min} by 1. ∎

Figure 3.2 shows an example execution of BLL on a labeled input graph satisfying AC. The ω value for chain $\langle D, 1, 2 \rangle$ appears above vertex 2, while the ω value for chain $\langle D, 3, 2 \rangle$ appears below vertex 2.

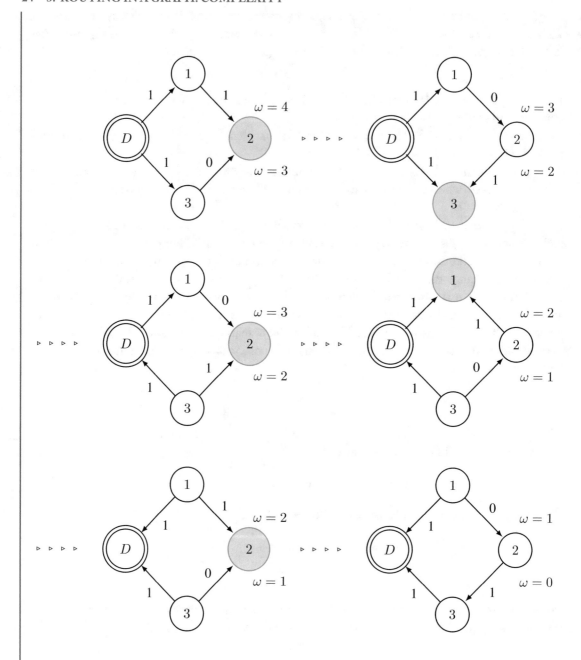

Figure 3.2: Example execution of BLL and evolution of work complexity quantities for vertex 2.

For BLL with the all-1's initial labeling (i.e., FR), every vertex v is in $\mathcal{N}$ initially, and for every chain from D to v, both *Res* and s are equal to 0. Thus we have:

Corollary 3.4   *Consider any execution of FR on input graph $\vec{G} = (V, \vec{E})$ and any $v \in V$. Then the work complexity of v, σ_v, is the minimum, over all chains from D to v of r, the number of links in the chain that are right-way (directed away from D).*

We can give an asymptotically tight bound of $\Theta(n_b^2)$ on the worst-case total work complexity of FR as a function of n_b, the number of bad vertices in the input graph, following the approach in [4, 5]. Since for each chain, r is at most n_b, $\sigma_v \leq n_b$ for any bad vertex v, and thus $\sigma = O(n_b^2)$. For the matching lower bound, consider the input graph

$$D \to v_1 \to \ldots \to v_{n_b} .$$

Since the work complexity of v_i is i, $1 \leq i \leq n_b$, the global work complexity for this input graph is $\Theta(n_b^2)$.

For BLL with the all-0's initial labeling (i.e., PR), every chain has $r = 0$, a sink vertex is in $\mathcal{S}$, a source vertex is in $\mathcal{N}$, and a vertex that is neither a sink nor a source is in $\mathcal{O}$. Thus, we have:

Corollary 3.5   *Consider any execution of PR on input graph $\vec{G} = (V, \vec{E})$ and any $v \in V$. If v is a sink or a source, then σ_v is the minimum, over all chains from D to v, of $s + Res$. Otherwise, σ_v is the minimum, over all chains from D to v, of $2s + Res$.*

We can also give an asymptotically tight bound of $\Theta(n_b^2)$ on the worst-case total work complexity of PR as a function of n_b, the number of bad vertices in the input graph, following the approach in [4, 5]. Since for each chain, s is at most n_b, $\sigma_v \leq n_b$ for any bad vertex v, and thus $\sigma = O(n_b^2)$. For the matching lower bound, consider the input graph that is a line with links alternating direction, that is,

$$D \to v_1 \leftarrow v_2 \to v_3 \leftarrow \ldots \to v_{n_b},$$

where n_b is odd[2]. For each vertex v_i, there is only one D-to-v chain and the value of s for this chain is approximately $i/2$, since the vertices with odd index are sinks. Thus the work complexity of v_i is $\Theta(i)$, and the global work complexity is $\Theta(n_b^2)$.

The foregoing analysis shows that in the worst case, the asymptotic work complexity of PR and FR are the same. This is perhaps counter-intuitive, as the idea of PR is to avoid reversing so many links.

---

[2]If n_b is even, then the rightmost link in the graph is outgoing from v_{n_b}.

3.1.3   FR VS. PR WITH GAME THEORY

As looking at worst-case graphs does not distinguish between the work complexity of FR and PR, Charron-Bost et al. [12] applied game theory to identify ways in which PR is cheaper than FR. The main results are that the work complexity of FR can be larger than the optimal work complexity by a $\Theta(|V|)$ factor, while the work complexity of PR is never more than twice the optimal.

Consider initial binary link labelings that are *locally uniform*, meaning that for each vertex, all incoming links have the same label. It is shown in [12] that any locally uniform labeling satisfies AC, and thus acyclicity is preserved by BLL using such initial labelings. Different locally uniform labelings give rise to different link reversal algorithms; FR and PR are extreme cases, being the all-1's and all-0's labelings, respectively.

We can view the construction of locally uniform labelings as a game in which each vertex is a *player* and the *strategy* of a player is the value, 0 or 1, with which it labels its incoming links. The game theory concepts (cf., e.g., [34]) defined next allow us to characterize the work complexity of a vertex based on its own labeling choice and those of the other vertices. Suppose the input graph is $\vec{G} = (V, \vec{E})$.

- A *profile* is a vector of strategies, one for each player in V.

- The *cost* incurred by a player v under profile $\vec{b}$, denoted $\sigma_v(\vec{b})$, is the work complexity of v in the BLL execution on $\vec{G}$ with initial labeling given by $\vec{b}$.

- Given profile $\vec{b}$, define profile $\vec{b}_{\overline{v}}$ to be the same as $\vec{b}$ except that v's strategy is $1 - \vec{b}[v]$. A profile $\vec{b}$ is a *Nash equilibrium* if, for each player v, the cost incurred by v under $\vec{b}$ is at most the cost incurred by v under profile $\vec{b}_{\overline{v}}$ i.e., $\sigma_v(\vec{b}) \leq \sigma_v(\vec{b}_{\overline{v}})$. Thus, no player has any incentive from a selfish viewpoint to change its strategy, assuming no other player changes its strategy.

- A profile $\vec{b}$ is a *global optimum* if each player incurs minimal cost. That is, for each player v and for each profile $\vec{a}$, $\sigma_v(\vec{b}) \leq \sigma_v(\vec{a})$.

- The *social cost* of profile $\vec{b}$ is the sum over all vertices v of $\sigma_v(\vec{b})$. This is the same as the global work complexity.

- The *minimum social cost* is the minimum, over all profiles, of the social cost incurred by that profile.

Let $\vec{1}$ be the all-1's profile (corresponding to FR) and let $\vec{0}$ be the all-0's profile (corresponding to PR).

The next Lemma states that if a player uses strategy 0, its cost will be at least as large as when it uses strategy 1, but no more than twice as large. The notation $\vec{b}_{v:i}$ means profile $\vec{b}$ with the entry for v replaced with i.

Lemma 3.6   *For every profile $\vec{b}$ and player v, $\sigma_v(\vec{b}_{v:1}) \leq \sigma_v(\vec{b}_{v:0}) \leq 2 \cdot \sigma_v(\vec{b}_{v:1})$.*

Proof. Suppose v is a source. Then v has no incoming links and its strategy is irrelevant to its work. Thus, $\sigma_v(\vec{b}_{v:0}) = \sigma_v(\vec{b}_{v:1})$.

Suppose v is not a source. Choose any D-to-v chain χ. Let ω^0 be $2(r^0 + s^0) + Res^0$, where r^0, s^0, and Res^0 are the values of r, s, and Res for chain χ under labeling $\vec{b}_{v:0}$. Similarly, let ω^1 be $2(r^1 + s^1) + Res^1$, where r^1, s^1, and Res^1 are the values of r, s, and Res for chain χ under labeling $\vec{b}_{v:1}$.

If the last link in χ is incoming to v, then $r^1 = r^0 + 1$, $s^1 = s^0$, and $Res^1 = Res^0 - 1$. The reason is that when v changes its strategy from 0 to 1, the value of r increases by 1 and Res goes from 1 to 0. Thus, $\omega^1 = \omega^0 + 1$. If the last link in χ is outgoing from v, then v's strategy is irrelevant to the values of r, s, and Res for χ, and thus $\omega^1 = \omega^0$.

Thus, for each D-to-v chain χ, in going from profile $\vec{b}_{v:0}$ to profile $\vec{b}_{v:1}$, the ω value for the chain is either the same or increases by 1. Thus, the minimum value of ω, over all D-to-v chains, either stays the same or increases by 1. That is, $\omega^0_{min} \leq \omega^1_{min} \leq \omega^0_{min} + 1$.

When v's strategy is 0, v is either in $\mathcal{S}$ (if v is a sink) or in $\mathcal{O}$ (if v is not a sink, since v is not a source). Thus, by Theorem 3.3, $\sigma_v(\vec{b}_{v:0})$ is either $(\omega^0_{min} + 1)/2$ or ω^0_{min}. Thus, $(\omega^0_{min} + 1)/2 \leq \sigma_v(\vec{b}_{v:0}) \leq \omega^0_{min}$.

When v's strategy is 1, v is in $\mathcal{N}$ since v is not a source, and by Theorem 3.3, $\sigma_v(\vec{b}_{v:1})$ is $\omega^1_{min}/2$. Thus, we have:

$$\begin{aligned} \sigma_v(\vec{b}_{v:1}) &= \omega^1_{min}/2 \\ &\leq (\omega^0_{min} + 1)/2 \\ &\leq \sigma_v(\vec{b}_{v:0}) \end{aligned}$$

and

$$\begin{aligned} \sigma_v(\vec{b}_{v:0}) &\leq \omega^0_{min} \\ &\leq \omega^1_{min} \\ &= 2 \cdot \omega^1_{min}/2 \\ &= 2 \cdot \sigma_v(\vec{b}_{v:1}). \end{aligned}$$

∎

The next Lemma states that, in contrast to the previous Lemma, if a player changes its strategy from 1 to 0, the cost incurred by any *other* player either stays the same or decreases.

Lemma 3.7   *For each profile $\vec{b}$ and all distinct vertices u and v, $\sigma_u(\vec{b}_{v:0}) \leq \sigma_u(\vec{b}_{v:1})$.*

Proof. If v is not on any D-to-u chain, then v's strategy has no effect on u's work. So suppose v is on such a chain, say χ. We consider the four cases, depending on the direction of the links of χ that are incident on v, and consider the effect on the ω value for χ when v's strategy changes from 1 to 0.

1. If both links are incoming to v, then s increases by 1 and r decreases by 1, resulting in no net change.

2. If both links are outgoing from v, then there is no effect.

3. If the link closer to D is incoming to v and that closer to u is outgoing from v, then r decreases by 1 and ω decreases by 2.

4. If the link closer to D is outgoing from v and that closer to u is incoming to v, then there is no effect.

In all cases, either ω stays the same or decreases for chain χ. Thus, the ω_{min} value for u either stays the same or decreases. Since changing v's strategy does not change whether u is in $\mathcal{S}, \mathcal{N}$, or $\mathcal{O}$, the work complexity of u either stays the same or decreases. That is, $\sigma_u(\vec{b}_{v:0}) \leq \sigma_u(\vec{b}_{v:1})$.   ∎

The next two Theorems summarize the key game-theoretic properties of $\vec{1}$ and $\vec{0}$.

Theorem 3.8 $\vec{1}$ is a Nash equilibrium. But $\vec{1}$ has the largest social cost among all Nash equilibria. In particular, the social cost of $\vec{1}$ can be larger than the minimum social cost by a factor that is linear in the number of vertices in the graph.

Proof.   We show that $\vec{1}$ is a Nash equilibrium (see [12] for proof of the other properties). Lemma 3.6 shows that, for each player v, $\sigma_v(\vec{1}_{v:1}) \leq \sigma_v(\vec{1}_{v:0})$. Since $\vec{1}_{v:1} = \vec{1}$, the result follows from the definition of Nash equilibrium.   ∎

Theorem 3.9 $\vec{0}$ is not necessarily a Nash equilibrium. But if $\vec{0}$ is a Nash equilibrium, then it is a global optimum and thus also has minimum social cost. Furthermore, the cost of $\vec{0}$ is never more than twice the minimum social cost.

Proof.   To show that $\vec{0}$ is not necessarily a Nash equilibrium, consider the chain

$$D \rightarrow u \leftarrow v \leftarrow w .$$

Under $\vec{0}$, player v's cost is 2, but if v changes its strategy to 1, then v's cost reduces to 1.

Next, we show that the cost of $\vec{0}$ is at most twice the minimum social cost. Suppose $\vec{c}$ is a profile with minimum social cost. One at a time, for each player v such that $\vec{c}[v] = 1$, consider the profile resulting from changing v's strategy from 1 to 0. By Lemma 3.6, v's cost at most doubles, and by Lemma 3.7, the cost of every other player either stays the same or decreases. After changing all the 1's to 0's, we obtain $\vec{0}$. Since the cost of each player at most doubles as compared with $\vec{c}$, the social cost of $\vec{0}$ is at most twice the minimum social cost.

See [12] for proof of the other properties.   ∎

The previous two theorems indicate a way in which PR is better than FR: the social cost incurred by PR is never more than twice the minimum social cost, whereas the social cost of FR can be larger than the minimum by a factor that depends on the size of the graph. So PR is a safe choice.

Another pleasing feature of PR is analyzed in [12]: When PR is executed on the result of disrupting a destination-oriented graph solely by the removal of some number of links, say k, each bad vertex incurs cost at most $2k$. In contrast, under FR even if just a single link is removed, a vertex can incur cost $|V| - 1$. This contained behavior of PR may be part of the reason it is the basis for several applications.

3.2   TIME COMPLEXITY

We measure the time complexity of LR as the number of iterations until termination. If the set of sinks scheduled to take steps is always of size 1, then the time complexity is the same as the global work complexity, which is the worst case. In this section, as in [4, 5], we focus on the time complexity in the more difficult case of *greedy* executions, where at each iteration, every vertex that is a sink takes a step. Such executions exhibit maximum concurrency. For each vertex, we count the number of iterations, or time steps, until the vertex has taken its last step. We assume that if a vertex is a sink at time t, then it takes a step at time $t + 1$; the initial state is time 0 and the first iteration occurs at time 1. For a given input graph, the iteration of the greedy execution at which vertex v takes its last step is denoted T_v, and is called the *time complexity* of v. The *global time complexity* is the maximum, over all vertices v, of T_v.

We analyze the FR case in Section 3.2.1; the general case of LR, which can be specialized to PR, is sketched in Section 3.2.2. This material is due to Charron-Bost et al. [9, 10].

3.2.1   FULL REVERSAL

We analyze the greedy execution of FR on input graph $\vec{G} = (V, \vec{E})$. For convenience, we let $V = \{0, 1, \ldots, n\}$, where 0 is the destination. For each vertex $v \in V$ and each time $t \geq 0$, let $\vec{W}_v(t)$ be the number of steps that v has taken up to and including time t; $\vec{W}_v(0)$ is defined to be 0. Note that σ_v, the work complexity of v, equals $\max\{\vec{W}_v(t) : t \geq 0\}$.

Lemmas 3.10 and 3.11 develop a recurrence relation for $\vec{W}_v(t)$, based on understanding how nodes and their neighbors take turns being sinks. A key observation is that this recurrence relation is linear in the min-plus algebra. Thus, as shown in Lemma 3.12, we can represent the set of recurrences for all the vertices as a matrix, which can be interpreted as the adjacency matrix of a graph $\vec{H}$ that is similar to $\vec{G}$. Lemma 3.13 restates the value of $\vec{W}_v(t)$ in terms of properties of paths in the new graph $\vec{H}$. Lemma 3.14 gives a formula for the limit of $\vec{W}_v(t)$ as t increases in terms of paths in $\vec{H}$; this result can be used to obtain an alternative proof of the work complexity of v since this limit is σ_v. Lemma 3.15 derives a formula for the time complexity T_v of vertex v based on properties of paths in $\vec{H}$. Finally, with the help of Lemma 3.14, Theorem 3.16 translates the results of Lemma 3.15 into properties of the original input graph $\vec{G}$.

Between any two consecutive steps of vertex v, each neighbor of v takes exactly one step. More precisely, for each vertex v, let In_v be $\{x \in N_G(v) : (x, v) \in \vec{E}\}$, the set of initially incoming neighbors of v, and let Out_v be $\{y \in N_G(v) : (v, y) \in \vec{E}\}$, the set of initially outgoing neighbors of v. Before v's first step (assuming it takes one at all), no vertex in In_v takes a step and every vertex in Out_v takes exactly one step.

We can deduce the following facts:

Lemma 3.10   *In the greedy FR execution, for every $v \in V$ and every $t \geq 0$,*

- $\vec{W}_v(t) \in \{\vec{W}_x(t) + 1, \vec{W}_x(t)\}$ *for all $x \in In_v$, and*

- $\vec{W}_v(t) \in \{\vec{W}_y(t), \vec{W}_y(t) - 1\}$ *for all $y \in Out_v$.*

Moreover, v is a sink at time t if and only if

- $\vec{W}_v(t) = \vec{W}_x(t)$ *for all $x \in In_v$, and*

- $\vec{W}_v(t) = \vec{W}_y(t) - 1$ *for all $y \in Out_v$.*

The next Lemma gives a recurrence relation on the number of steps taken by a vertex and its neighbors.

Lemma 3.11   *In the greedy FR execution,*

- $\vec{W}_v(0) = 0$ *for all $v \in V$,*

- $\vec{W}_0(t) = 0$ *for all $t \geq 0$, and*

- $\vec{W}_v(t + 1) = \min\{\vec{W}_x(t) + 1, \vec{W}_y(t) : x \in In_v, y \in Out_v\}$ *for all $v \in V \setminus \{0\}$ and all $t \geq 0$.*

Proof.   Since initially no node has taken a step, $\vec{W}_v(0) = 0$ for all $v \in V$, and since vertex 0 never takes a step, $\vec{W}_0(t) = 0$ for all $t \geq 0$.

For the third bullet, we first consider the case when $v \in V \setminus \{0\}$ is a sink at time t. Since the execution is greedy and v is not 0, $\vec{W}_v(t + 1) = \vec{W}_v(t) + 1$. By Lemma 3.10, $\vec{W}_v(t) = \vec{W}_x(t)$ for all $x \in In_v$, and thus $\vec{W}_v(t + 1) = \vec{W}_x(t) + 1$ for all $x \in In_v$. Similarly, we can argue that $\vec{W}_v(t + 1) = \vec{W}_v(t) + 1 = \vec{W}_y(t) - 1 + 1 = \vec{W}_y(t)$ for all $y \in Out_v$. Thus, the desired equality holds.

Now we consider the case when v is not a sink at time t. Thus $\vec{W}_v(t + 1) = \vec{W}_v(t)$.

First, we show that $\vec{W}_v(t + 1) \leq \min\{\vec{W}_x(t) + 1, \vec{W}_y(t) : x \in In_v, y \in Out_v\}$. By Lemma 3.10, $\vec{W}_v(t) \leq \vec{W}_x(t) + 1$ for all $x \in In_v$, and $\vec{W}_v(t) \leq \vec{W}_y(t)$ for all $y \in Out_v$, and thus the desired upper bound on $\vec{W}_v(t + 1)$ holds.

Now we show that $\vec{W}_v(t + 1) \geq \min\{\vec{W}_x(t) + 1, \vec{W}_y(t) : x \in In_v, y \in Out_v\}$. By Lemma 3.10, it is not the case that $\vec{W}_v(t) = \vec{W}_x(t)$ for all $x \in In_v$ and $\vec{W}_v(t) = \vec{W}_y(t) - 1$

for all $y \in Out_v$. Suppose there exists $x_0 \in In_v$ such that $\vec{W}_v(t) \neq \vec{W}_{x_0}(t)$. By Lemma 3.10, it follows that $\vec{W}_v(t) = \vec{W}_{x_0}(t) + 1$, and thus the desired lower bound on $\vec{W}_v(t+1)$ holds.

If such an x_0 does not exist, then there must be a $y_0 \in Out_v$ such that $\vec{W}_v(t) \neq \vec{W}_{y_0}(t) - 1$. By Lemma 3.10, it follows that $\vec{W}_v(t) = \vec{W}_{y_0}(t)$, and thus the desired lower bound on $\vec{W}_v(t+1)$ holds. ∎

The recurrence relation in the previous lemma gives rise to a discrete linear dynamical system in min-plus algebra [21]. In min-plus algebra, given an $m \times p$ matrix M and a $p \times q$ matrix N, define $M \otimes N$ as the $m \times q$ matrix whose (i, j)-th entry is defined to be $\min\{M_{i,k} + N_{k,j} : 0 \leq k < p\}$. Note that the operator $\otimes$ is associative.

In our particular situation, let A be the $(n+1) \times (n+1)$ matrix whose (v, u)-th element, $0 \leq v, u \leq n$, is defined to be 1 if $u \in In_v$, to be 0 if $u \in Out_v$ or if $v = u = 0$, and to be ∞ otherwise. We can then restate Lemma 3.11 as follows (A^t denotes $A \otimes A \otimes \cdots \otimes A$ with A appearing t times):

Lemma 3.12   *In the greedy FR execution, for every $t \geq 0$, $\vec{W}(t) = A^t \otimes \vec{0}$, where $\vec{0}$ is the column vector of $n+1$ 0's.*

Proof.   We use induction on t. For the base case, when $t = 0$, $\vec{W}(0) = \vec{0} = A^0 \otimes \vec{0}$. For the inductive case, we assume the equality is true for t and show it is true for $t + 1$.

$$
\begin{aligned}
A^{t+1} \otimes \vec{0} &= A \otimes A^t \otimes \vec{0} && \text{since } \otimes \text{ is associative} \\
&= A \otimes \vec{W}(t) && \text{by the inductive hypothesis} \\
&= C,
\end{aligned}
$$

where C is an $(n+1)$-size column vector whose v-th entry is $\min\{A_{v,u} + \vec{W}_u(t) : 0 \leq u < n+1\}$. It follows from the definition of $A_{v,u}$ that $C_v = \min\{\vec{W}_x(t) + 1, \vec{W}_y(t) : x \in In_v, y \in Out_v\}$, which, by Lemma 3.11, equals $\vec{W}_v(t+1)$. Thus, C equals $\vec{W}(t+1)$. ∎

A can be viewed as the adjacency matrix of a directed, weighted[3] graph that is related to $\vec{G}$, which we call the *in-out graph*, denoted $\vec{H}$. $\vec{H}$ has the same set of vertices, V, as $\vec{G}$. For each link (u, v) in $\vec{G}$, $\vec{H}$ has two links, (u, v) and (v, u), (u, v) weighted with $A_{v,u}$ and (v, u) weighted with $A_{u,v}$. That is, for each link in $\vec{G}$, there are two links in $\vec{H}$; the link in $\vec{H}$ that goes in the same direction as in $\vec{G}$ is weighted with 1, while the link going in the opposite direction is weighted with 0. There is also a self-loop on vertex 0 with weight 0. See Figure 3.3 for an example.

We can now characterize $\vec{W}_v(t)$ in terms of paths in $\vec{H}$. Given a path π, let $len(\pi)$ be the length of the path (the number of links in the path), and let $wt(\pi)$ be the weight of the path (the sum of the weights on all the links in the path). Let $\mathcal{P}_{*,v}$ be the set of all paths in $\vec{H}$ that end at vertex v. The next Lemma shows that in the greedy FR execution, $\vec{W}_v(t)$ is the minimum weight of all paths in $\vec{H}$ that end at v and have length t.

Lemma 3.13   *In the greedy FR execution, for every $v \in V$ and every $t \geq 0$, $\vec{W}_v(t) = \min\{wt(\pi) : \pi \in \mathcal{P}_{*,v} \text{ and } len(\pi) = t\}$.*

---

[3] The link weights of $\vec{H}$ are not related to the link labels of BLL.

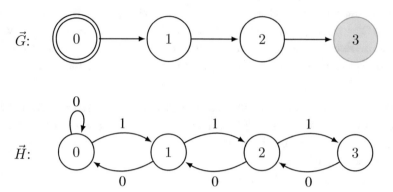

Figure 3.3: Example of directed graph $\vec{G}$ and its in-out graph $\vec{H}$.

Proof. Fix v and t. By Lemma 3.12, $\vec{W}(t) = A^t \otimes \vec{0}$. By definition of $\otimes$ and $\vec{0}$, $\vec{W}_v(t) = \min\{A^t_{v,u} : u \in V\}$. A straightforward induction shows that

$$A^t_{v,u} = \min\{A_{v,x_1} + A_{x_1,x_2} + \cdots + A_{x_{t-1},u} : x_1, x_2, \ldots, x_{t-1} \in V\}.$$

The sequence of vertices $\langle u, x_{t-1}, x_{t-2}, \ldots, x_2, x_1, v \rangle$ forms a path in $\vec{H}$ that ends at v, i.e., is in $\mathcal{P}_{*,v}$, has length t, and has minimum weight of all such paths.   ∎

Let $\mathcal{P}_{0,v}$ denote the set of all paths in $\vec{H}$ that start at vertex 0 and end at vertex v. The next Lemma gives a formula for the limit of $\vec{W}_v(t)$ as t increases in terms of $\mathcal{P}_{0,v}$. This limit is the work complexity σ_v of vertex v. (This Lemma provides an alternate way of computing the work complexity of FR as compared to Section 3.1.2.)

Lemma 3.14   *In the greedy FR execution, for every vertex v,*

$$\lim_{t \to \infty} \vec{W}_v(t) = \min\{wt(\pi) : \pi \in \mathcal{P}_{0,v}\}.$$

Proof. Fix v. Since $\vec{H}$ is strongly connected, there is a path from 0 to v. Let π be such a path with the minimum weight. Let $t_0 = len(\pi)$ and $z_0 = wt(\pi)$. By Lemma 3.13, $\vec{W}_v(t_0) \leq z_0$.

For each $t > t_0$, we can create a path from 0 to v of length t and with the same weight z_0, by prepending to π the necessary number of copies of the self-loop on vertex 0. Thus, $\vec{W}_v(t) \leq z_0$ for all $t \geq t_0$. Since $\vec{W}_v$ is nondecreasing, the sequence $\{\vec{W}_v(t)\}_{t \geq 0}$ is stationary and its limit is at most z_0.

We now show that this limit is at least z_0. Suppose not. Then there is a time t_1 and a value $z_1 < z_0$ such that for all $t \geq t_1$, $\vec{W}_v(t) = z_1$. By Lemma 3.13, for all $t \geq t_1$, there is a path π_t in

$\mathcal{P}_{*,v}$ with length t and weight z_1. Path π_t cannot include vertex 0, otherwise its weight would be at least z_0, since weights are nonnegative and z_0 is the minimum weight of any path from 0 to v. But since $\vec{G}$ is acyclic, all cycles in $\vec{H}$ that exclude vertex 0 have positive weight, so the weight of paths excluding vertex 0 with larger and larger length must have weight that eventually exceeds z_0. ∎

The next Lemma characterizes the time complexity as a function of paths in the in-out graph $\vec{H}$. As mentioned earlier, good vertices take no steps. The Lemma shows that a bad vertex v takes its last step at the iteration whose index is one larger than the length of the longest path in the in-out graph ending at v whose weight is one less than v's work complexity.

Lemma 3.15 *In the greedy FR execution, for any bad vertex $v \in V$, the termination time T_v is $1 + \max\{len(\pi) : \pi \in \mathcal{P}_{*,v}$ and $wt(\pi) = \sigma_v - 1\}$.*

Proof. Since vertex v's last step is at time $T_v \geq 1$, it follows that $\vec{W}_v(T_v) = \vec{W}_v(T_v - 1) + 1$. Thus, $\vec{W}_v(T_v - 1) = \sigma_v - 1$.

Let $\mathcal{Q}$ be the set of paths in $\mathcal{P}_{*,v}$ with weight $\sigma_v - 1$. By Lemma 3.13, there is a path in $\mathcal{Q}$ of length $T_v - 1$. So the maximum length of any path in $\mathcal{Q}$ is at least $T_v - 1$, i.e., $T_v \leq 1 + \max\{len(\pi) : \pi \in \mathcal{Q}\}$.

Now we show the other direction. By Lemma 3.13, any path in $\vec{H}$ that ends at v and has length exactly T_v must have weight at least σ_v. Since weights are nonnegative, it follows that any path in $\vec{H}$ that ends at v and has length T_v or longer must have weight at least σ_v. Thus, each path in $\vec{H}$ that ends at v and has weight less than σ_v must have length less than T_v. So $\max\{len(\pi) : \pi \in \mathcal{Q}\} \leq T_v - 1$, which implies that $T_v \geq 1 + \max\{len(\pi) : \pi \in \mathcal{Q}\}$. ∎

Finally, we can restate the previous lemma in terms of the original graph $\vec{G}$ instead of the in-out graph $\vec{H}$:

Theorem 3.16 *In the greedy FR execution, for every bad vertex $v \in V$, the termination time T_v is $1 + \max\{len(\chi) : \chi$ is a chain in $\vec{G}$ ending at v with $r = \sigma_v - 1\}$.*

Proof. Consider any path π in $\mathcal{P}_{*,v}$ with $wt(\pi) = \sigma_v - 1$.

We first argue that π cannot contain vertex 0. If, in contradiction, π contains vertex 0, then there is a suffix π' of π that starts at 0 and ends at v, i.e., is in $\mathcal{P}_{0,v}$. By Lemma 3.14, $wt(\pi')$ would have to be at least as large as σ_v, and since $wt(\pi)$ must be at least as large as $wt(\pi')$, this is a contradiction.

Since π does not contain vertex 0, it has no occurrences of the self-loop on vertex 0 in $\vec{H}$. Thus, the sequence of vertices that make up π form a chain χ in $\vec{G}$; χ also ends at vertex v and has the same length as π. A link with weight 1 (resp., 0) in π corresponds to a right-way (resp., wrong-way) link in χ. Thus, the value of r for χ equals $wt(\pi)$, which is $\sigma_v - 1$. ∎

The global time complexity, denoted T_{fin}, is the time of the last step of any vertex, and equals $\max\{T_v : v \in V\}$. Following the approach first proposed by Busch et al. [4, 5], we can give a tight asymptotic bound on the worst-case value of T_{fin} as a function of the input graph $\vec{G}$. Let n_b be the number of bad vertices in $\vec{G}$ and recall that only bad vertices take steps. Since the work complexity of any vertex is at most n_b, the total number of steps taken is at most n_b^2. Since at least one step is taken at each time, $T_{fin} = O(n_b^2)$.

We now show that for every value of n_b, there exists a graph with n_b bad vertices for which T_{fin} is $\Omega(n_b^2)$. Consider the graph[4] consisting of a chain $\langle 0, 1, \ldots, k\rangle$, followed by a circuit $\langle k, k + 1, \ldots, n_b, k\rangle$ (see Figure 3.4). In the chain, each link is oriented from smaller to larger endpoint. In the circuit, each link is oriented from larger to smaller endpoint. The work complexity, σ_k, of vertex k is k. The chain consisting of $k - 1$ copies of the circuit $\langle k, k + 1, \ldots, n_b, k\rangle$ ends at k, has $\sigma_k - 1 = k - 1$ right-way links (directed toward k), and has length $(k - 1)(n_b - k + 1)$. By Theorem 3.16, $T_k = (k - 1)(n_b - k + 1)$. By setting $k = \lfloor n_b/2 \rfloor$, we get that T_k, and thus T_{fin}, are $\Omega(n_b^2)$.

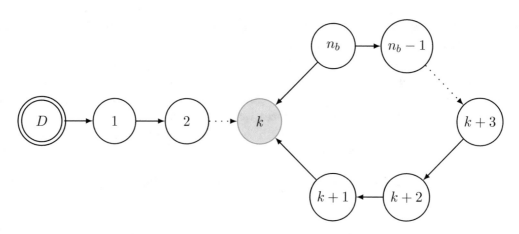

Figure 3.4: A graph on which FR has quadratic global time complexity.

3.2.2   GENERAL LR AND PARTIAL REVERSAL

To analyze the time complexity of the general LR algorithm, including PR as a special case, Charron-Bost et al. [10] transformed link-labeled input graph $\vec{G}^\ell$ into an (unlabeled) directed graph $T(\vec{G}^\ell)$. The transformation ensures that for every execution of LR on $\vec{G}^\ell$, there is a corresponding execution of FR on $T(\vec{G}^\ell)$. Furthermore, the time complexities of relevant vertices in the corresponding executions are the same.

[4]An alternative graph is given in [4, 5]: instead of a circuit at the end of the chain, there is a clique. The argument proceeds by noting that all reversals done by vertices in the clique must occur sequentially.

The key observation is that if a vertex v is initially in the category $\mathcal{O}$ (a sink with a mix of marked and unmarked incident links, or not a sink and has an unmarked incoming link), then its incident links are partitioned into two sets. All the links in one set reverse at odd-numbered steps by v, while all the links in the other set reverse at even-numbered steps by v. In contrast, vertices that are not in $\mathcal{O}$ reverse all their incident links at each step, which is FR-like behavior. The transformation replaces each vertex v in $\mathcal{O}$ with two vertices, one corresponding to odd steps by v and the other to even steps, and inserts appropriate links.

The formula obtained in this way for the time complexity of PR is the following:

Theorem 3.17 In the greedy PR execution, for every bad vertex $v \in V$, the termination time T_v is:

- $1 + \max\{len(\chi) : \chi$ is a chain ending at v with $s + Res = \sigma_v - 1\}$ if v is a sink or a source initially, and

- $1 + \max\{len(\chi) : \chi$ is a chain ending at v with $2s + Res = \sigma_v - 1\}$ if v is neither a sink nor a source initially.

Similarly as for FR, we can show an upper bound of $O(n_b^2)$ on the worst-case global termination time for PR: the global time complexity cannot exceed the global work complexity, which is $O(n_b^2)$. For a matching lower bound, consider the following chain graph on vertices 0 through n, where n is even and $\frac{n}{2}$ is odd, and the links in the left half of the chain alternate direction, while those in the right half are all directed away from 0.

$$0 \to 1 \leftarrow 2 \to 3 \leftarrow \ldots \to \frac{n}{2} \to \frac{n}{2} + 1 \to \ldots \to n$$

Vertex $\frac{n}{2}$ is neither a sink nor a source, so by Corollary 3.5 its work complexity is $\frac{n}{2}$. To compute the time complexity of $\frac{n}{2}$, consider the chain χ that starts at $\frac{n}{2}$, ends at $\frac{n}{2}$, and goes back and forth between vertices $\frac{n}{2}$ and n making $\frac{n-2}{4}$ round trips. The chain χ has $\frac{n-2}{4}$ sinks in it (due to the $\frac{n-2}{4}$ occurrences of vertex n) and $Res = 0$, so $2s + Res$ for this chain is $\frac{n}{2} - 1$, which is one less than the work complexity of vertex $\frac{n}{2}$. Since the length of χ is $\frac{n-2}{4} \cdot n$, Theorem 3.17 implies that the time complexity of vertex $\frac{n}{2}$ is at least $\frac{n-2}{4} \cdot n = \Omega(n^2)$.

Interestingly, the global time complexity of FR on this graph is only linear in n (and in fact it is shown in [9] that FR has linear global time complexity on any tree). Calculations in [10] determine that on this graph PR has smaller work complexity than FR ($\frac{5}{16}n^2 + \frac{1}{4}n + \frac{1}{4}$ vs. $\frac{5}{16}n^2 + \frac{3}{4}n + \frac{1}{4}$). Thus on this graph, FR has significantly better global time complexity than PR but somewhat worse global work complexity.

CHAPTER 4

Routing and Leader Election in a Distributed System

In this section, we consider how link reversal ideas similar to those presented in the previous section have been used in distributed applications. We focus on systems in which the computing nodes communicate through message passing, especially systems in which the communication topology changes dynamically. We discuss two applications of link reversal in such systems: routing and leader election. For both applications, the goal is to ensure that a specific unchanging node is the unique sink (either globally or in its connected component). First, we describe our model of computation in Section 4.1. Section 4.2 presents an algorithm called TORA for routing in mobile ad hoc networks, in which the communication topology changes dynamically. In Section 4.3 we discuss adaptations of TORA for the problem of leader election in dynamic networks.

4.1   DISTRIBUTED SYSTEM MODEL FOR APPLICATIONS

We now present a more detailed model for distributed systems. The general idea is to identify a computing node (or processor) with each vertex in the graph and to consider each graph edge as a communication channel. However, there are several aspects of distributed systems that were not accounted for in the previous section's approach to link reversal. These include:

- How do two neighboring nodes know which way the link between them should be directed? The nodes will presumably need to communicate by sending messages, and these messages can be subject to delays (and perhaps even loss).

- In systems in which nodes move, the communication topology—and thus the graph—changes dynamically. In fact, the topology is not necessarily connected.

For the applications, we will assume the following system model. There is a collection of n processing nodes that communicate with each other through message passing. The communication can be either through wired or wireless means. An undirected graph models the ability of nodes to communicate directly with each other: if nodes i and j can communicate directly with each other, then there is an edge between the vertices corresponding to i and j. We do not consider the possibility of one-way communication.

In several cases, we consider the possibility that nodes move; for instance, this is the case in a mobile ad hoc network. Node mobility naturally affects the communication graph, and thus we model the communication graph as a function of real time. We assume that some lower-level "neighbor discovery" protocol takes care of determining which nodes are within communication range of each other, and indicates this information to the endpoints of the links with LinkUp and LinkDown events (cf., e.g., [13]).

We assume that messages sent over a link that remains up are delivered exactly once, without corruption, and in the order in which they are sent, and that only messages previously sent are delivered. Different assumptions can be made about what happens to messages that are in transit when a link goes down. Unless stated otherwise, we will assume that these messages are lost. We assume that nodes never experience any faults.

An *execution* of an algorithm in the distributed system model is a sequence of the form $\langle C_0, e_1, C_1, e_2, C_2, \ldots \rangle$, where each C_k is a *configuration* (snapshot of the current states of all the nodes and all the communication channels) and each e_k is an event that cause a processor to take a step (such as the receipt of a message or some internal action). C_0 is an *initial* configuration, in which the nodes are in initial states and the channels are empty. Each event e_k is *enabled* in the preceding configuration and the following configuration correctly reflects the changes brought about by e_k.

4.2   ROUTING IN DYNAMIC GRAPHS

One drawback of the routing algorithms in the previous section is that vertices that are partitioned from the destination never terminate. The absence of a vertex that never takes a step causes the other vertices to do infinitely many reversals. See the example for FR in Figure 4.1. In a distributed implementation, this means that the nodes never stop sending messages, which wastes communication bandwidth. (In contrast, Section 8 considers an application in which non-termination is useful, namely resource allocation.)

Informally, a routing algorithm for dynamic graphs should ensure the following two properties in all executions with a finite number of changes to the communication topology. Let D be the destination node. (1) After the last topology change, every node that is in the same connected component as D (with respect to the undirected communication graph) eventually has a path to D (with respect to some orientation of the communication graph). (2) After the last topology change, every node that is not in the same connected component as D stops doing any work related to finding a route to D or sending a message to D.

4.2.1   OVERVIEW OF TORA

Park and Corson [35] developed a routing algorithm to satisfy these goals. The algorithm is based on the Increasing Vertex Labels algorithm of Gafni and Bertsekas [19] (cf. Algorithm 4). In the new algorithm, the node labels, called *heights*, are 5-tuples. As in IVL, the new algorithm ensures that every node in the same connected component as the destination eventually has a path to the destination in the orientation of the communication graph induced by the heights. Furthermore, by clever use of the additional entries in the height structure, the algorithm is able to identify when nodes have been partitioned from the destination; these nodes can then stop wasting resources searching

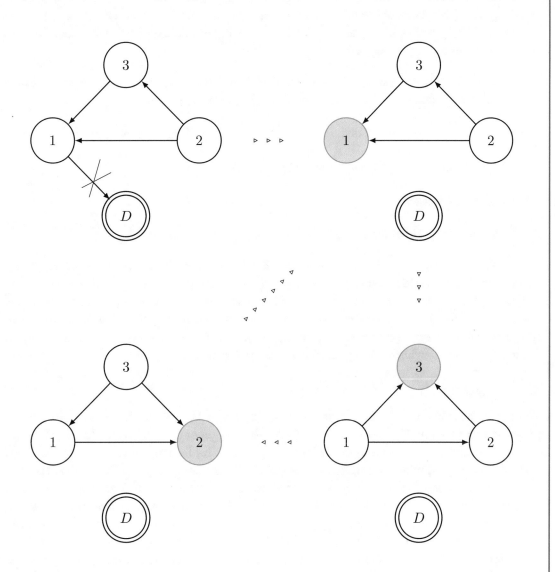

Figure 4.1: Example execution of FR when the graph is partitioned: When the link between node 1 and D goes away, node 1 becomes a sink, then 3 becomes a sink, then 2 becomes a sink, then 1 becomes a sink again, etc.

for a (non-existent) path to the destination. This algorithm is called TORA, for Temporally Ordered Routing Algorithm, because one of the new entries in the heights contains time values.

In TORA, the height h of a node consists of a 5-tuple ($tau, oid, rbit, delta, id$). The first three components comprise the *reference level*.

- *tau* is either 0 or a timestamp that records the time when this reference level was created; nodes are assumed to have access to perfectly synchronized clocks.

- *oid* is either 0, or is the id of a node called the *originator* of the reference level.

- *rbit* is the *reflection bit* of the reference level and is either 0 or 1.

- *delta* is an integer.

- *id* is the unique id of the node.

As with the Pair and Triple algorithms, each link is considered to be directed from the endpoint with larger height to that with smaller, where heights are compared lexicographically; heights of different nodes are always unique, since node ids are used as tie-breakers (in the least-significant location). Each node keeps track of what it thinks is the current height of each of its neighbors; this information is exchanged by sending messages. Since messages are subject to arbitrary delays, a node's view of the heights of its neighboring nodes can be out of date.

4.2.2   ROUTE CREATION

Park and Corson [35] described an initialization procedure for TORA, starting with a global state in which the destination D has height $(0, 0, 0, 0, D)$, each neighbor of D knows the height of D, and no other heights are yet assigned, either for a node itself or for its neighbors. When a node needs to find a route to D, it broadcasts a query message, which is then propagated through the network until reaching a node that has a height assigned to itself. In response to a query message, a node with a height assigned to itself broadcasts its height in an update message. Each recipient of an update message that is in need of a height adopts the reference level of the received height, and sets its *delta* to be one larger than the *delta* of the received height. In this way nodes also learn about the heights of their neighbors. The paper does not explicitly address what happens if topology changes occur during the route creation procedure.

Assuming no topology changes occur during route creation, at the end of this procedure, every node has a height for itself and knows the heights of all its neighbors. The heights all have reference level (0,0,0) and the *delta* values ensure that every node has a directed path to the destination. Subsequent topology changes are handled via a route maintenance procedure, pseudocode for which is given in Algorithm 6 and explained next.

4.2.3 ROUTE MAINTENANCE

Suppose a link goes down (Lines 1-6 in Algorithm 6) at node i. If i becomes a singleton node, then i is partitioned from the destination and starts erasing routes to D in a manner that is explained in Section 4.2.4. Otherwise, no action is taken unless i is now a sink, according to its view of its neighbors' heights. If i is a sink, then it begins a search for a new path to the destination. This search is tagged with a new reference level which consists of the current time (*tau*); the id of this node (*oid*), which is the originator of the new reference level; and reflection bit 0 (*rbit*). Then i broadcasts its new height to all its neighbors. This effects a full reversal, since *tau* is the most significant component in the heights for the comparison, and, by the assumption of perfect clocks, all the neighbors have a smaller *tau* value than the new one just chosen by i to be the current time.

The purpose of the reflection bit is to keep track of whether the search is spreading outward from the originator—in which case the bit is 0—or if the search has hit a dead end at some node and is being reflected back to the originator—in which case the bit is 1. The *delta* variable is manipulated in such a way to keep the links pointing away from the originator while the search is spreading outward, and pointing toward the originator while the search is reflecting back.

If a node i becomes a sink because it receives a message containing a new height for a neighbor j, i takes one of the following actions:

- (Lines 11-12) If i's neighbors have different reference levels, then i propagates the largest reference level by taking on the largest neighboring reference level, and setting its *delta* to be one less than the smallest *delta* value among all the neighbors with the largest reference level. This effects a partial reversal, since all links to nodes with the largest reference level remain incoming while all links to nodes with smaller reference levels, of which there is at least one, become outgoing.

- (Lines 13-14) If all i's neighbors have the same unreflected reference level (*rbit* is 0), then i is a dead-end for this search. It reflects this reference level by taking on the same *tau* and *oid* values but setting *rbit* to 1; the *delta* value is set to 0. This effects a full reversal.

- (Lines 15-16) If all i's neighbors have the same reflected reference level (reflection bit is 1), and i was the originator of this reference level, then all of i's attempts to find a new path to D have failed and been reflected back. Node i has now detected that it is partitioned from D; its subsequent actions are explained in Section 4.2.4.

- (Line 17) If all i's neighbors have the same reflected reference level, but i was *not* the originator of this reference level, then something has been disrupted due to node mobility, and i starts a new reference level.

Whenever i changes its height, i broadcasts its new height (Lines 6 and 18). When a link comes up (Lines 19–20), the nodes exchange height information in messages over the link; clearly this will not cause any node to lose an existing path to the destination.

Algorithm 6: Route Maintenance in Temporally Ordered Routing Algorithm (TORA);
code for node $i \neq D$

---

1 **when** LinkDown event occurs for link to node j:
2   remove j from *Neighbors*
3   **if** *Neighbors* $= \emptyset$ **then** ** partition detected **
4   **else if** `Sink()` **then**
5   `StartNewRefLevel()`
6   broadcast *height*[i]
7

8 **when** height message h is received from node j:
9   *height*[j] $:= h$
10   add j to *Neighbors*
11   **if** `Sink()` **then**
12   **if** not all neighbors' reference levels are the same **then**
13   `PropagateLargestRefLevel()`
14   **else if** common neighbors' reference level has $h.rbit = 0$ **then**
15   `ReflectRefLevel(`h`)`
16   **else if** common neighbors' reference level has $h.oid = i$ **then**
17   ** partition detected **
18   **else** `StartNewRefLevel()`
19   broadcast *height*[i]
20

21 **when** LinkUp event occurs for link to node j:
22   send *height*[i] to j

23 `Sink()`:
24   **return** (*height*[i] $<$ *height*[j] for all $j \in$ *Neighbors*)

25 `StartNewRefLevel()`:
26   *height*[i] $:= (time, i, 0, 0, i)$

27 `PropagateLargestRefLevel()`:
28   *height*[i]$.rl :=$ largest among neighbors' reference levels
29   *height*[i]$.delta :=$ one less than smallest delta among all neighbors' with largest reference level

30 `ReflectRefLevel(`h`)`:
31   *height*[i] $:= (h.tau, h.oid, 1, 0, i)$

4.2.4   ERASING ROUTES

When a node i detects that it has been partitioned from the destination (Lines 3 and 16 of Algorithm 6), it starts erasing the routes to that destination as follows. First, i broadcasts a clear message which contains the destination's id as well as the reflected reference level that caused the detection; i also empties its set of neighbors. When a node i receives a clear message with the same reference level as its own, it clears its height, empties the neighbor set, and rebroadcasts the clear message. When a node i receives a clear message with a different reference level than its own, it removes the sender of the clear message from its neighbor set, but apparently does not rebroadcast the clear.

4.2.5   DISCUSSION

The description of TORA given above assumes that nodes have perfectly synchronized clocks. This assumption ensures that the mechanism for directing the links using the *tau* values, which are timestamps, works properly. Park and Corson [35] pointed out that all that is necessary, though, are logical clocks [28], which are integer counters that respect causality. If the *tau* values do not respect causality, Park and Corson stated that correctness is maintained but "the efficiency with which routes are reestablished" is impaired [35].

To argue that TORA is correct, Park and Corson [35] appealed to the correctness proof by Gafni and Bertsekas [19] for the generic height-based algorithm (cf. Theorem 2.9), as the rules by which nodes change their heights in TORA during route maintenance can be shown to satisfy the requirements. This is a possible direction for showing that nodes ultimately in the same connected component as D obtain a path to D. Two discrepancies between the model assumed for Theorem 2.9 and the model for which TORA is proposed need to be addressed, though, in order to complete such an argument. The first discrepancy is the instantaneous knowledge of neighbors' heights vs. the asynchronous delay of height messages. The second discrepancy is the static nature of the graph vs. the occurrence of multiple topology changes. Furthermore, Theorem 2.9 does not address the correctness of the partition-detection functionality in TORA, nor of the route creation and route erasure procedures.

An alternate approach to proving the correctness of TORA is to adapt the proof of the leader election algorithm [26] presented next, which is a modification of TORA. This idea is discussed in the next subsection.

4.3   LEADER ELECTION IN DYNAMIC GRAPHS

A well-known problem in distributed systems is that of *leader election*. Roughly speaking, a leader election algorithm should choose exactly one node in the system, the "leader". This unique node can then perform actions on behalf of the entire system. Some applications that need a leader include the primary-backup approach to fault-tolerance using replication, video-conferencing, and multi-player games.

When the communication graph can change dynamically, it makes more sense to elect a leader in each connected component, assuming a group of nodes form one connected component sufficiently long. This particular version of the leader election problem was dubbed the "local leader election problem" by Fetzer and Cristian [18].

TORA, the routing algorithm for dynamic graphs, can be adapted to solve this leader election problem. The first attempt was by Malpani et al. [31], and it works as long as there is only a single topology change (one link going down or coming up) at a time.

In Lines 3 and 16 in Algorithm 6, a node detects that it is partitioned from the destination. The key observation for converting TORA into a leader election algorithm, is to view the destination as the leader. Thus, Lines 3 and 16 indicate that the node has been partitioned from its (old) leader. A new leader is needed for the newly created connected component, so this node elects itself.

Once a node has elected itself, the id of the new leader needs to be propagated throughout the connected component. Also, if two connected components with different leaders join into one component, then the disagreement over the leaders needs to be resolved. These problems are taken care of by propagating leader information throughout the connected component using a "wave" algorithm [39].

These changes can be implemented within the height framework of TORA, by adding an additional, sixth, component, the leader id. A correctness proof is given in [31], but it assumes synchronous message delays.

Subsequent work by Ingram et al. [26] extended the leader election algorithm to handle multiple arbitrary topology changes. A seventh component is added, a timestamp on the leader id. The wave algorithm for dealing with conflicting leader ids now works correctly even when multiple topology changes occur. This paper includes a detailed proof of correctness for the asynchronous message delay case.

The correctness proof for the algorithm in [26] has two main parts. The first part shows that after the last topology change, each connected component is a "leader-oriented DAG", i.e., every node in the component knows that one particular node in the component, say ℓ, is the leader, and the direction of links induced by the heights causes ℓ, and only ℓ, to be a sink. In more detail, it is shown that after the last topology change, each node in the component elects itself a finite number of times and a finite number of new reference levels are started. These observations imply that eventually no messages are in transit. At that point, the DAG is leader-oriented. The second part of the analysis attempts to show that a new leader is not elected "unnecessarily", i.e., under certain situations, the algorithm will ensure that nodes that have lost a directed path to the existing leader will find an alternate path to the pre-existing leader, rather than electing a new leader. We conjecture that the first part of the proof for the leader election algorithm can be simplified to show the correctness of TORA's partition detection mechanism. Furthermore, the second part of the proof—regarding not electing a new leader unnecessarily—may be relevant to showing that TORA does not falsely detect partitions [36].

CHAPTER 5

Mutual Exclusion in a Distributed System

In this section, we consider algorithms based on link reversal ideas that solve the mutual exclusion problem. Like routing algorithms, these algorithms ensure that there is only one sink at a time in the system, but the sink can move, meaning that different nodes in the system can be the unique sink at different times (it does not refer to physical movement of the sink node). We use the same model for distributed systems as in Section 4.1. The bulk of the section focuses on an algorithm for static networks (Section 5.1), followed in Section 5.2 by a discussion of adaptations for dynamic networks.

5.1 MUTUAL EXCLUSION IN FIXED TOPOLOGIES

We first define the *mutual exclusion* problem for distributed networks [39]. Each node runs an application process that has a special section of code called its *critical section*. When an application process wants to enter its critical section, it should eventually be allowed to do so; however, no two application processes should be in their critical sections at the same time. While an application process is waiting to enter its critical section, it is said to be in its *waiting* section. While a node is not concerned with the critical section, it is said to be in its *remainder* section.

Each node runs a mutual exclusion (mutex) process (cf. Figure 5.1). The mutex and application processes on the same node cooperate so that the application process cycles between its remainder section, its waiting section (triggered by RequestCS from the application process), its critical section (triggered by EnterCS from the mutex process), and then back to its remainder section (triggered by ReleaseCS from the application process), in that order. The set of mutex processes communicate with each other by message passing over the network to synchronize when the application processes are allowed to enter their critical sections. The mutex processes together must ensure that in every execution[1]:

Exclusion Condition: At most one process is in its critical section, at every point in the execution.

Fairness Condition: Every process requesting access to the critical section eventually enters the critical section.

---

[1] Recall that executions for the distributed system model are defined at the end of Section 4.1.

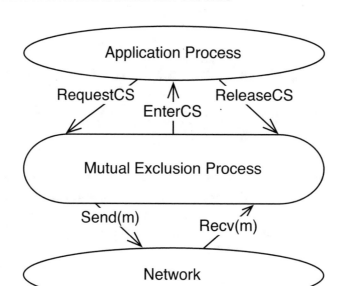

Figure 5.1: System Architecture.

5.1.1   LRME ALGORITHM

In the late 1980's, three similar algorithms [32, 38, 40] were developed independently by three different teams for using link reversal to solve the mutual exclusion problem in static distributed systems. We give a short overview of these algorithms first, and then present one of them in detail. Hélary et al. [22] provided a formal framework for describing distributed mutual exclusion algorithms that operate by forwarding a token over a tree; their framework includes as special cases all three of these algorithms.

Naimi and Trehel [32] presented an algorithm for a clique communication topology that uses two distributed data structures: a queue of waiting processes such that each process knows only the next process in the queue, and a rooted directed tree overlay which indicates the path over which a request is forwarded to reach the tail of the queue. When a request is forwarded, the virtual direction of the link is reversed. As shown by Naimi et al. [33], the expected message complexity of this algorithm is $O(\log n)$ per critical section entry.

The first algorithm discussed by Snepscheut [40] assumes the network topology is a tree. Exclusion is ensured by maintaining exactly one token in the system, which is circulated via messages among the nodes of the tree. A requesting node can enter the critical section only if it has the token. Logical directions are imposed on the communication links of the tree so as to ensure that the node currently possessing the token is the only sink; since the topology is a tree, a node that does not have the token has exactly one outgoing link; which is in the direction of the node that has the token.

When a node enters the waiting section, it sends a "request" message on its unique outgoing link, i.e., toward the token. The recipient of a "request" message forwards the message on its own unique outgoing link if it is not already waiting for the token; in any case it keeps track of the sender of the "request" message. When the token-holder finishes executing in the critical section, it sends the token to one of its neighbors that is waiting for the token; a simple approach is for each node to keep a FIFO queue of neighbors that have sent it an as-yet unanswered "request" message. If the node still has unanswered requests, it sends a "request" message after the token. When the token traverses a link, the direction of the link reverses to point toward the new token-holder.

Now suppose the network topology is an arbitrary connected graph. The algorithm just described could be adapted to this case by running it on a spanning tree of the arbitrary graph. However, this approach does not take full advantage of the additional links in the graph, which can be used to provide shorter paths and some redundancy in case of lost links. Instead, Snepscheut describes a modification to the tree algorithm that works as long as the initial topology is a directed acyclic graph (DAG), with the token-holder being the unique sink. The main differences are: (1) a request message can be forwarded on any outgoing link; and (2) when a node receives the token, *all* its outgoing links are reversed to become incoming.

Raymond [38] gave an expanded version of the spanning-tree-based algorithm from [40], including more details for the code and for the correctness proof. She also described an extension of the algorithm that tolerates failures and recoveries of nodes.

Below we present a more detailed version of the DAG-based algorithm from [40]—which we call LRME for "Link-Reversal Mutual Exclusion"—and a correctness proof, using ideas from [38] and [42]. See Algorithm 7 for pseudocode. Each node i has a local variable $status_i$ that cycles between the values REMAINDER, WAITING, and CRITICAL, depending on which mutual exclusion section its application process is in; initially, $status_i$ is REMAINDER. The local variable N_i holds the ids of all of i's neighbors in the communication topology graph.

To manage the token, each node i has a local variable $hasToken_i$, which is true if and only if i has the token. To manage the link directions, each node i keeps two local variables, OG_i and IC_i, which contain the ids of the neighbors of i that are considered to be outgoing and incoming respectively. We assume that these variables are initialized so that the $hasToken$ variable of exactly one node in the network is true, the two endpoints of each link have a consistent view of the direction of that link, and globally the directions induce a token-oriented DAG.

When node i receives a message containing the token, it sets $hasToken_i$ to true and reverses the directions of all its outgoing links so that i is now a sink. The mechanism for the link reversal is a message handshake: i sends a *MakeOG* message to each node j that is an outgoing neighbor of i, instructing j to move i from IC_j to OG_j. When j has done so, it sends an acknowledgment message *AckOG* to i. Once i has received all the acknowledgments, i puts all its neighbors in IC_i and empties OG_i. While waiting for the acknowledgments, i takes no other actions.

To ensure fair access to the critical section, each node has a local variable RQ (for "request queue"), which is initially empty. When a node i wishes to enter the critical section, it enqueues its own id in RQ_i. Similarly, when a node i receives a *Request* message from an (incoming) neighbor j, it enqueues j in RQ_i. In both cases, if the newly enqueued element is the only element in i's request queue, then i sends a *Request* message to any one of its outgoing neighbors; otherwise it sends no request message, relying instead on a previously sent request message (to lure the token to i).

A node i that currently has the token calls HandleToken() in three situations: (1) if i receives a request message while it is not in the critical section; (2) if i enters the waiting section; or (3) if i leaves the critical section and i's request queue is non-empty. In each of these cases, i dequeues the request queue. If the result is its own id, then i enters the critical section. Otherwise, i sends the token in a message to the neighbor whose id was just dequeued; if i's request queue is still not empty, then i sends a request message after the token (so that the token will return to i in the future).

Discussion of link reversal aspects of the algorithm: The virtual direction on the link between two nodes is implemented with the *IC* and *OG* sets and link direction is reversed by the handshaking between the two endpoints of a link via the *MakeOG* and *AckOG* messages. Unlike the algorithms in the previous sections, neither link labels nor height labels are employed. Another important difference is that a node that receives the token makes itself become a sink; in contrast, in the previous algorithms a node that becomes a sink because of the behavior of its neighbors makes itself become a non-sink.

5.1.2   CORRECTNESS OF LRME ALGORITHM

We now argue why the LRME algorithm is correct. Consider any arbitrary execution of the algorithm (subject to our usual constraints that messages are not lost, etc., listed in Section 4.1) in which the application processes behave "properly". By "properly", we mean that at each node, the application process interacts with the mutex process so that the remainder-waiting-critical cycle is respected, and the application process never stays in the critical section forever. We will show that in this execution, exclusion and fairness are satisfied.

First, the exclusion property follows from parts (a) and (d) of the following Lemma. The proof is by induction; the other parts are needed to make the induction go through, and some are used later as well.

Lemma 5.1   *In every configuration of the execution, the following are true:*

(a) At most one process has hasToken *equal to true.*

(b) If no process has hasToken *equal to true, then there is exactly one* Token *message in transit.*

(c) If any process has hasToken *equal to true, then there is no* Token *message in transit.*

(d) If process i has status$_i$ = CRITICAL, *then* hasToken$_i$ = *true.*

(e) If status$_i$ = WAITING, *then i appears exactly once in* RQ_i.

(f) If status$_i$ *is not* WAITING, *then i is not in* RQ_i.

Algorithm 7: Link Reversal Mutual Exclusion (LRME) Algorithm for Static Networks;
code for node i

---

 1 **when** *Request* message received from node j:
 2   Enqueue(RQ, j)
 3   **if** *hasToken* **then**
 4   **if** *status* $\neq$ critical **then** HandleToken()
 5
 6   **else if** $|RQ| = 1$ **then**
 7   send *Request* message to arbitrary $k \in OG$
 8

 9 **when** *Token* message received from node j:
10   *hasToken* := true
11   send *MakeOG* message to all $k \in OG$
12   wait for *AckOG* message from all $k \in OG$
13      $IC := N; OG := \emptyset$
14   **if** $|RQ| > 0$ **then** HandleToken()

15 **when** *MakeOG* message received from node j:
16   remove j from IC and add to OG
17   send *AckOG* message to j

18 **when** Application requests access to critical section (RequestCS):
19   *status* := WAITING
20   Enqueue(RQ, i)
21   **if** *hasToken* **then** HandleToken()
22   **else if** $|RQ| = 1$ **then**
23   send *Request* message to arbitrary $k \in OG$
24

25 **when** Application releases critical section (ReleaseCS):
26   *status* := REMAINDER
27   **if** $|RQ| > 0$ **then** HandleToken()

28 HandleToken():
29   p := Dequeue(RQ)
30   **if** $p \neq i$ **then**
31   *hasToken* := false
32   send *Token* message to p
33   **if** $|RQ| > 0$ **then** send *Request* message to p
34
35   **else** *status* := CRITICAL (EnterCS)

Proof. These properties can be shown by induction on the sequence of configurations in the execution.

In the initial configuration, $hasToken$ is true for exactly one process and no messages are in transit, so (a) is true, (b) is vacuously true, and (c) is true. Also, in the initial configuration, for every process i $status_i$ is REMAINDER and RQ_i is empty, so (d) and (e) are vacuously true and (f) is true.

For the inductive step, suppose the t-th configuration (referred to as the "old" configuration) satisfies the properties. We must consider all possibilities for the event that leads to the $t + 1$-st configuration (called the "new" configuration). Here, we give one case in detail; the rest are proved similarly. We use the notation IH(a) to refer to the inductive hypothesis for part (a), etc.

- Node i receives a *Request* message from node j. The properties are only affected if procedure HandleToken is executed. By Lines 3-4, HandleToken is only called if, in the old configuration, $hasToken_i$ is true and $status_i$ is not CRITICAL.

  Case 1: Lines 28-29 are executed. Then $hasToken_i$ is set to false and a *Token* message is sent.

  By IH(a), i is the only node with $hasToken$ true in the old configuration, so in the new configuration, no node has $hasToken$ true. Thus part (a) is true in the new configuration.

  By IH(c), no *Token* message is in transit in the old configuration, so only one *Token* message is in transit in the new configuration. Thus part (b) is true in the new configuration.

  Part (c) is vacuously true in the new configuration since no process has $hasToken$ equal to true.

  Part (d) is vacuously true in the new configuration since $status_i$ is not CRITICAL.

  Since the item dequeued from RQ_i is not i (cf. Line 27), and $status_i$ is not changed, (e) and (f) are not affected. Thus IH(e) and IH(f) imply that parts (e) and (f) are true in the new configuration.

  Case 2: Lines 28-29 are not executed. Then Line 31 is executed, meaning that $status_i$ is set to CRITICAL.

  Since no change is made to $hasToken_i$, part (a) is true in the new configuration because of IH(a).

  Part (b) is vacuously true in the new configuration.

  Since no *Token* message is sent, part (c) is true in the new configuration because of IH(c).

  Part (d) is true in the new configuration since $status_i$ is set to CRITICAL and $hasToken_i$ remains true.

  Part (e) is vacuously true in the new configuration.

  Line 31 is executed because i is in RQ_i in the old configuration. So by IH(f), $status_i$ is WAITING in the old configuration. By IH(e), that is the only occurrence of i in RQ_i in the old configuration. Thus in the new configuration, i is not in RQ_i, and part (f) is true.

- Node i receives a *Token* message from node j. By IH(c), in the old configuration no process has *hasToken* true since there is a *Token* message in transit. And by IH(b), since there are no *hasToken* variables that are true, there is at most one *Token* message in transit. Also, by IH(d), since *hasToken$_i$* is false in the old configuration, *status$_i$* is not CRITICAL in the old configuration. The rest of the argument proceeds by considering several cases: whether or not HandleToken is called, and in case it is, whether or not Lines 28–29 are executed.

- Receipt of *MakeOG* or *AckOG* message: Neither causes any changes that are relevant to the properties.

- Application process requests access to CS at i: We are assuming that the application behaves properly, so in the old configuration, *status$_i$* is REMAINDER. By IH(f), i is not in RQ_i in the old configuration. After Lines 17-18, *status$_i$* = WAITING and one copy of i is in RQ_i. The rest of the argument proceeds by considering several cases: whether or not *hasToken$_i$* is true in the old configuration, and in case it is, whether or not Lines 28–29 of HandleToken are executed.

- Application process indicates transition to remainder section: Since we are assuming the application process behaves properly, in the old configuration, *status$_i$* is CRITICAL. Thus, in the old configuration: by IH(d), *hasToken$_i$* = true; by IH(c), no *Token* message is in transit; and by IH(f), i is not in RQ_i. The rest of the argument proceeds by considering two cases, whether or not RQ_i is empty.

∎

Theorem 5.2   The LRME algorithm satisfies exclusion.

Proof. Since a process i is in the critical section only if *hasToken$_i$* is true, the proof follows from Lemmas 5.1(a) and (d). ∎

To prove the fairness property, we consider the chain of requests initiated by a node in its waiting section and show that the token travels around the network, causing the requests to move to the heads of their respective queues, so that eventually the waiting node is allowed to enter the critical section. This intuition is formalized using a variant function.

In more detail, we first define a node as the token-holder if, roughly speaking, it either has, or is about to have, the token. We then argue in Lemma 5.3 about the consistency with which neighboring nodes view the direction of the link between them, and based on this result, we define an orientation of the communication topology graph. Using basic properties of link reversal, we show in Lemma 5.4 that this directed graph is always a DAG in which the token-holder is the only sink.

In order to continue, we need several invariant properties relating to request queues, which are presented in Lemma 5.5. A key property among these invariants, which is related to link reversal, is that if i is in the request queue of j, then (i, j) is in the directed graph. Next, we define the concept of "request chain", which captures the idea that i sends a request to j, j sends a request to k, etc., until the token-holder is reached. Based on the invariant properties, Lemma 5.6 shows that the request chain is bounded and has no repeats; this follows from the fact that the directed graph has no cycles. Finally we define a function and show in Lemma 5.7 that it satisfies the properties of a variant function. Theorem 5.8 wraps up the argument.

A node i is said to be a *token-holder* in a configuration if either $hasToken_i = true$ or a *Token* message is in transit to i from a neighbor of i.

By Lemma 5.1, parts (a), (b) and (c), there is a unique token-holder in every configuration.

We next show that the two endpoints of a link have a consistent view of the direction of the link as long as neither endpoint is the token-holder. If one endpoint is the token-holder, then after the token-holder has received the *Token* message and exchanged *MakeOG* and *AckOG* messages with its neighbors—that is, before it calls `HandleToken`—the token-holder and its neighbors also have consistent views. For brevity, we say i and j are *link-consistent* if either $i \in OG_j$ and $j \in IC_i$, or $i \in IC_j$ and $j \in OG_i$.

Lemma 5.3   *Let i and j be neighboring nodes.*

(a) *If neither i nor j is the token-holder, then i and j are link-consistent.*

(b) *If i is the token-holder and has finished Line 11 since becoming the token-holder, then i and j are link-consistent.*

Proof.   The proof is by induction on the sequence of configurations in the execution. The basis follows from the definition of the initial configuration. For the inductive step, we assume the properties are true in the t-th configuration and consider what can occur when transitioning to the $(t + 1)$-st configuration. The properties are affected by anything that changes which node is the token-holder or that changes the OG or IC set of a node.

Suppose the token-holder changes. This is caused by the old token-holder i sending a *Token* message on Line 29, in `HandleToken`, to node j. By part (b) of the inductive hypothesis, i and each of its neighbors is link-consistent in the old configuration. Thus, part (a) is true in the new configuration considering i and each of its neighbors other than j. Part (b) is vacuously true in the new configuration with respect to j since j has not yet reached Line 11.

Now suppose the OG or IC set of a node i changes. This only occurs in Lines 11 and 14, as part of the message handshake between a node that just received the *Token* message and its neighbors. The recipient of a *MakeOG* message is a neighbor of the token-holder and the result is for the recipient to direct the link toward the token-holder. The sender of the *MakeOG* message is the token-holder; it changes the direction of all its outgoing links simultaneously after receiving the last *AckOG* message. Thus, changes to OG or IC do not affect part (a). Before the token-holder reaches Line 11, part (b) is vacuously true, and once the token-holder executes Line 11, it is link-consistent with all its neighbors. ∎

Recall that $G = (V, E)$ is the undirected graph that models the static bidirectional communication topology of the network. For each configuration C_t of the execution, we define an orientation of G, called $\vec{G}_t$, as follows. The set of vertices of $\vec{G}_t$ is V, the same as in G. The directed link (i, j) is in $\vec{G}_t$ if and only if i and j are neighbors in G, and one of the following two conditions is true in C_t:

- j is the token-holder, or

- neither i nor j is the token-holder, and $j \in OG_i$. (By Lemma 5.3(a), it is also true that $i \in IC_j$.)

$\vec{G}_t$ is said to be *token-oriented* if the token-holder is the only sink in C_t.

Lemma 5.4   *For every configuration C_t of the execution, $\vec{G}_t$ is a token-oriented DAG.*

Proof.   The proof is by induction on the sequence of configurations in the execution. For the basis, the initialization assumptions give the result. For the inductive step, we assume $\vec{G}_t$ is a token-oriented DAG and show the same is true of $\vec{G}_{t+1}$, no matter which event occurs between C_t and C_{t+1}.

$\vec{G}_{t+1}$ differs from $\vec{G}_t$ only if the token-holder changes. Suppose in the event between C_t and C_{t+1} node i sends a *Token* message to its neighbor j, in HandleToken. Then the token-holder changes from i in C_t to j in C_{t+1}. By Lemma 5.3, i is link-consistent with each of its neighbors in C_t. Thus, for each neighbor k of i other than j, the link between i and k does not change direction in going from C_t to C_{t+1}. All the links incident on j become incoming to j in $\vec{G}_{t+1}$, i.e., j is a sink. The only sink in the previous configuration was i, so in the new configuration, j is the only sink. The changes to the link directions in going from $\vec{G}_t$ to $\vec{G}_{t+1}$ do not cause a cycle because only links incident on j change direction. So if a cycle were to be created, it would have to include j. But j is a sink and cannot be part of a cycle.   ∎

The next Lemma states some additional invariants that are needed to show the fairness condition of the algorithm. They can be proved by induction similarly to the proof of Lemma 5.1.

Lemma 5.5   *The following are true in every configuration C_t of the execution.*

(a) *If $i \in RQ_j$ or a* Request *message is in transit from i to j, then $(i, j) \in \vec{G}_t$.*

(b) *Suppose $|RQ_i| > 0$ and i is not the token-holder. Then there is a neighbor j of i such that exactly one of the following holds: (i) exactly one* Request *message is in transit from i to j, and i is not in RQ_j, or (ii) no* Request *message is in transit from i to j, and exactly one copy of i is in RQ_j. Further, for every neighbor k of i other than j, there is no* Request *message in transit from i to k, and i is not in RQ_k.*

(c) *If $|RQ_i| = 0$, then there is no* Request *message in transit from i and i is not in the request queue of any of its neighbors.*

(d) If i is the token-holder, then i is not in the request queue of any of its neighbors, and no Request *message is in transit from i. Further, if* hasToken$_i$ *is true, then i is not in its own request queue.*

Given a configuration, a *request chain* for any node l is a maximal length sequence of node identifiers $\langle p_1, p_2, \ldots, p_m \rangle$, such that $i = p_1$ and $p_\ell \in RQ_{p_{\ell+1}}$ for each ℓ, $1 \le \ell < m$.

Note that if node i has an empty request queue, then its request chain is the empty sequence, denoted $\langle \rangle$.

Lemma 5.6   *In every configuration C_t of the execution, there is exactly one request chain for each node i and it contains no repeated ids.*

Proof.   By Lemma 5.5(b), if a node i has a nonempty request queue, then at most one of its neighbors has i in its request queue. Thus, there is exactly one request chain for a given node.

Let $\langle p_1, p_2, \ldots, p_m \rangle$ with $i = p_1$ be the request chain for node i. By Lemma 5.5(a), $(p_\ell, p_{\ell+1})$ is a directed link of $\vec{G}_t$, for each ℓ, $1 \le \ell < m$. Since $\vec{G}_t$ is acyclic by Lemma 5.4, there can be no repeated ids in the request chain.   ∎

Consider any configuration in the execution. Let i be a node with request chain $\langle p_1, p_2, \ldots, p_m \rangle$ where $i = p_1$. A function V_i for i is defined to be the following vector of positive integers. V_i has either $m + 1$ or m elements $\langle v_1, v_2, \ldots \rangle$, depending on whether a *Request* message is in transit from p_m or not. In either case, v_1 is the position of $p_1 = i$ in RQ_i, and for $1 < \ell \le m$, v_ℓ is the position of $p_{\ell-1}$ in RQ_{p_ℓ}. (Positions are numbered in ascending order with 1 being the head of the queue.) If a *Request* message is in transit from p_m, then V_i has $m + 1$ elements and $v_{m+1} = n + 1$; otherwise, V_i has only m elements. In the following lemma, we show that if these vectors are compared lexicographically, V_i is a variant function.

Lemma 5.7   *For each node i, V_i is a variant function.*

Proof.   By Lemma 5.6, V_i never has more than n entries. Suppose an entry in V_i is the position of an element in a request queue. By Lemma 5.5(b), each id appears at most once in a request queue, so the maximum value of such an entry in V_i is n. By the definition of V_i, then, every entry is between 1 and $n + 1$.

Next, we show that the value of V_i never increases. We consider all the possible events that can affect V_i. If $i = p_1, p_2, \ldots, p_m$ is i's request chain in configuration C_t of the execution, then we must consider the cases when the next event

- adds p_m to a request queue, or

- removes p_ℓ from a request queue, for any ℓ, $1 \le \ell < m$, or

- changes the position of p_ℓ in the request queue of $p_{\ell+1}$, for any ℓ, $1 \le \ell < m$.

Suppose p_m is added to a neighboring node j's request queue. This is due to the receipt at j of a *Request* message from p_m. The value of V_i thus decreases from $\langle v_1, \ldots, v_m, n+1 \rangle$ to $\langle v_1, \ldots, v_m, v'_{m+1} \rangle$, where $v'_{m+1} < n+1$ since v'_{m+1} is p_m's position in RQ_j after the *Request* message is received.

Suppose p_ℓ is removed from a request queue, for some ℓ, $1 \le \ell \le m$. Only the token-holder removes items from its request queue. Because of Lemma 5.5(d), if the token-holder is in a request chain, it must be the last element. Thus, $\ell = m - 1$. So p_{m-1} is removed from the request queue of p_m and p_m sends a *Token* message to p_{m-1}. This causes p_m to become the new token-holder. The request chain shrinks by dropping the last element, and V_i decreases from $\langle v_1, \ldots, v_{m-1}, v_m \rangle$ to $\langle v_1, \ldots, v_{m-1} \rangle$.

Suppose the position of p_ℓ in the request queue of $p_{\ell+1}$ changes, for some ℓ, $1 \le \ell < m$. Because the request queues are FIFO, enqueueing of elements does not change the position of pre-existing entries. So it must be the dequeueing of an element that changes p_ℓ's position; this change is a decrease by 1. As argued in the previous paragraph, p_m is the node doing the dequeueing and p_m is the token-holder. Let j be the id that was dequeued. Then p_m sends a *Token* message to j, immediately followed by a *Request* message. Thus, V_i decreases from $\langle v_1, \ldots, v_{m-1}, v_m \rangle$ to $\langle v_1, \ldots, v_{m-1}, v_m - 1, n+1 \rangle$.

We have shown that any event that changes V_i must decrease it. Now we show that events are guaranteed to keep occurring until V_i decreases to the minimum value of $\langle \rangle$.

Suppose in contradiction that V_i reaches a value larger than $\langle \rangle$ in some configuration of the execution and it never changes thereafter. This means that the request chain for node i stops changing. Look at the last node, p_m, in the final request chain. By the definition of request chain, none of p_m's neighbors has p_m in its request queue, but p_m has a nonempty request queue.

Case 1: p_m is the token-holder, and thus is not i. But p_m eventually stops being the token-holder, since it is not in the critical section forever and it has a nonempty request queue. When p_m leaves the critical section, its request queue is dequeued and so V_i changes, a contradiction.

Case 2: p_m is not the token-holder. Since p_m is the end of the request chain, Lemma 5.5(b) implies that a *Request* message is in transit to some neighbor of p_m. When this message is delivered, the request chain lengthens and V_i changes, a contradiction.   ∎

Theorem 5.8   The LRME algorithm guarantees fairness.

Proof.   Suppose i is a node that starts requesting entry to the critical section at some time. By the code, i enters its id in its request queue; now V_i is nonempty and the first element is the position of i in RQ_i. By Lemma 5.7, at some later time V_i is the empty sequence $\langle \rangle$. This means that i has dequeued its own id from its request queue and entered the critical section.   ∎

5.2 MUTUAL EXCLUSION FOR DYNAMIC TOPOLOGIES

The algorithm given in the previous subsection is not guaranteed to work correctly if the network topology changes. One difficulty arises when links go down. The DAG-based algorithm is arguably more robust to links going down than the spanning-tree-based algorithm, but it is still possible to disconnect the network. Even if the network is not disconnected, the DAG-based algorithm experiences difficulty in the following case: Suppose j is in node i's request queue, but then the link between i and j goes down. Then i will not know to which neighbor the token should be forwarded. Another difficulty is how to assign directions to new links that come up so that a cycle is not created. If a cycle were created, then there is no guarantee that requests will reach the token-holder. Suppose for instance that i sends a request to j, j sends a request to k, and k sends a request to i, while the token remains at some fourth node m which never learns about the requests from i, j, and k.

To overcome these difficulties, Dhamdhere and Kulkarni [16], building on work by Chang et al. [8], proposed an extension to Raymond's tree-based algorithm that exploits multiple outgoing links and handles links going down and coming up. A dynamically changing sequence number is assigned to each node such that the token-holder always has the highest sequence number and links are directed from lower to higher sequence numbers. Thanks to the sequence numbers, there is no ambiguity as to which way a new link should be directed, and cycles cannot be formed. If a node becomes a sink due to link failures, flooding is used to build a temporary spanning tree over which this node sends a high priority request to the token-holder. Under the assumption that there is an upper bound on the number of link failures, the higher priority requests will not cause starvation of other requests.

Walter et al. [42] observed that the difficulties caused by link failures and recoveries can be overcome in a more uniform way by adding vertex labels to the Snepscheut mutual exclusion algorithm RLME presented in Section 5.1.1 for a static network. The vertex labels are triples, similar to those used in the Triple routing algorithm from Section 2.2; the first two components are integers that change while the third component is the node's id. When a node receives the token, it changes its height to be lower than that of the previous token-holder, and thus lower than that of any node in the system, by adopting the first two components of the previous token-holder and then decrementing the second component by 1. If a node i becomes a sink because of the loss of an outgoing link (either the link goes away or the link becomes incoming due to the change of the label at the other end), i raises its height similarly to the Triple algorithm in Section 2.2: i sets the first component of its triple to be one larger than the smallest first component of all its neighbors' triples; let x denote the new value of the first component of i's triple. Then i sets the second component of its triple to be one less than the smallest second component of all its neighbors' triples whose first component equals x. Whenever loss of a link or a change in link direction causes a node j to cease being an incoming neighbor of i, the entry for j (if any) is purged from i's request queue. After a node raises its height, if the purged request queue is still non-empty, then a new "request" message is sent over an outgoing link.

Walter et al. [42] provided a detailed proof of correctness of the algorithm. The exclusion condition is proved using the same observations as for the RLME algorithm: there is never more than one token-holder at a time, and a node enters its critical section only if it is the token-holder. To prove the fairness condition, it is first assumed that the token message is never lost, in spite of link failures. Consider a connected component of the graph that contains the token and experiences no further topology changes. Then it is proven that nodes in that connected component raise their heights a finite number of times. Once nodes stop raising their heights, it is shown that the component forms a token-oriented DAG, and then fairness can be shown along the same lines as for RLME in Section 5.1.1.

CHAPTER 6

Distributed Queueing

The three mutual exclusion algorithms discussed in Section 5.1.1 [32, 38, 40] all keep track of a distributed queue that determines the order in which requesting processors enter the critical section. Demmer and Herlihy [15] focused on the queueing aspect of these algorithms, and called their presentation the Arrow protocol. In this algorithm, each node in the system can request to join a total order. The ordering is calculated in a distributed way, and each node ultimately learns just its successor in the ordering, but not the entire ordering. In Section 6.1, we define the distributed queueing problem and describe the Arrow protocol, following Herlihy et al. [23]. Section 6.2 contains a correctness proof. We conclude in Section 6.3 with a discussion of other analyses of the Arrow protocol that have been presented in the literature.

6.1   THE ARROW PROTOCOL

Let $G = (V, E)$ be a connected undirected graph with no self-loops modeling the communication topology of the system. Let r_0 be a distinguished node in V. Each node, other than r_0, can experience as an input at most one "queueing request" event. Each node i has a local variable $succ_i$. Given an execution, let A be the set of nodes consisting of r_0 and all nodes that experience a queueing request. Define a binary relation $<$ on A as follows: for all nodes i and j with $i \neq j$, if $succ_i = j$, then $i < j$. An algorithm that solves the *distributed queueing problem* sets the values of the $succ_i$ variables such that eventually the relation $(A, <)$ is a total order.

The Arrow protocol operates on a fixed spanning tree $T = (V, E_T)$ of G. Each node i has a variable $succ_i$, which holds either $\perp$ or the id of a node in V (not necessarily a neighbor). Each node i also has a variable $parent_i$, which holds either its own id i, or the id of a neighboring node in T. Let $\vec{T}$ be the directed graph whose vertex set is V and whose link set contains the directed link (i, j) iff $parent_i = j$, for all i and j in V.

In the initial configuration of the algorithm, $succ_i = \perp$ for each node i. The $parent_i$ variables are set initially so that $\vec{T}$ is an r_0-oriented tree: there is a self-loop on r_0 and every other node has a path to r_0.

The distributed queue is considered to hold r_0 initially; this is why we assume that r_0 never experiences a queueing request. The algorithm handles queueing requests by building up longer and longer total orders by appending one total order to another. Each node that is a sink in $\vec{T}$ is the tail of a total order. Initially, there is just one total order and r_0 is its tail (as well as its head). When a node experiences a queueing request, it sends a message to its parent in $\vec{T}$ requesting to be enqueued and becomes its own parent, i.e., a sink. When a node i receives such a message on behalf of, say, node k, if i is a sink, i.e., the tail of a total order, then i enqueues k immediately after itself, by setting $succ_i$ equal to k. This has the effect of appending k's total order to the end of i's total order. If i, the recipient of the message, is not a sink, it forwards the message to its parent in $\vec{T}$ and then changes its parent to be the sender of the message, thus *reversing the link* between the sender and recipient of the message. See Algorithm 8 for the pseudocode.

Algorithm 8: Arrow Distributed Queueing Algorithm; code for node i

---

1 **when** a queueing request occurs:
2   send $enq(i)$ to *parent*
3   *parent* $:= i$

4 **when** $enq(k)$ message received from node j:
5   **if** *parent* $= i$ **then**
6 | $succ := k$
7   **else** send $enq(k)$ to *parent*
8   *parent* $:= j$

Figures 6.1 and 6.2 show an example execution. The solid arrows represent the current state of $\vec{T}$; a dotted line indicates an edge that is in T but not in $\vec{T}$.

6.2   CORRECTNESS OF ARROW

We now prove that the Arrow protocol is correct. We consider an arbitrary execution of the protocol in which each node experiences a queueing request at most once, and r_0 never does. For each configuration in the execution, define A, the set of *active* nodes, to consist of r_0 and every node that has experienced a queueing request previously.

The next Lemma states some basic properties about active and inactive nodes.

Lemma 6.1   *Consider any configuration of the execution.*

(a) *For every active node $i \neq r_0$, either there exists exactly one node j such that $succ_j = i$ and no $enq(i)$ message is in transit, or there is no node j such that $succ_j = i$ and exactly one $enq(i)$ message is in transit.*

(b) *For every inactive node i (which by definition is not r_0),*

   (i) *there is no node j such that $succ_j = i$, and*

   (ii) *there is no $enq(i)$ message in transit, and*

   (iii) *$succ_i = \perp$, and*

   (iv) *$parent_i \neq i$.*

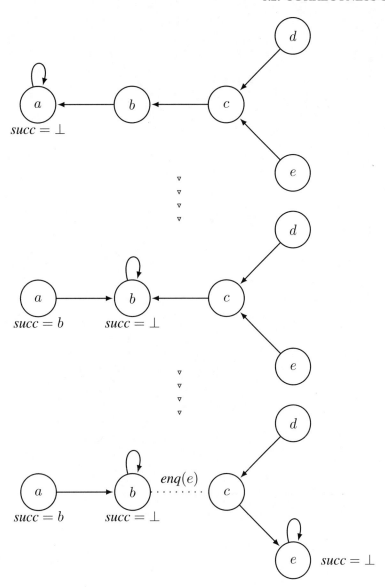

Figure 6.1: The top graph is the initial state; the relation is [*a*]. The middle graph is the result of node *b* enqueueing itself: *b* sends a message to *a* and becomes its own parent; node *a* receives the message, sets its successor to *b*, and makes *b* its parent; the relation is now [*a*, *b*]. The bottom graph shows an intermediate state while node *e* is being enqueued: *e* sends a message to its current parent *c* and becomes its own parent; *c* gets the message, forwards the message to its current parent *b*, and makes *e* its new parent; the message from *c* to *b* is in transit; the relation is now [*a*, *b*], [*e*].

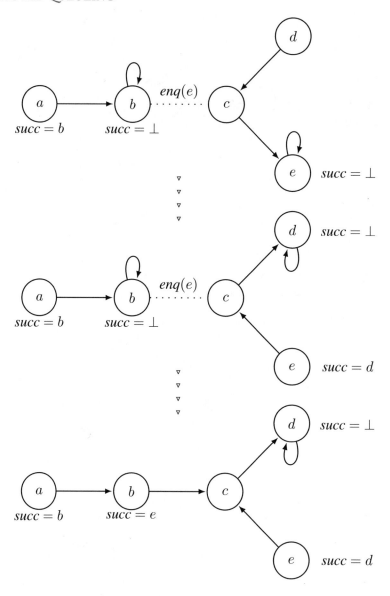

Figure 6.2: The top graph is a repeat of the bottom graph from the previous figure. The middle graph shows an intermediate result while node d is being enqueued: d sends a message to its current parent c and becomes its own parent; c gets the message, forwards the message to its current parent e, and makes d its new parent; e gets the message from c and sets its successor to d and its parent to c; the relation is now $[a, b]$, $[e, d]$. The bottom graph shows the final result: b receives the message from c regarding e and sets its successor to e and its parent to c; the final relation is the total order $[a, b, e, d]$.

(c) For every node i (including r_0), if $parent_i = i$, then $succ_i = \perp$.

Proof. The proof is by induction on the configurations of the execution. Initially, $A = \{r_0\}$, and for every node i, $succ_i$ is $\perp$, and no messages are in transit. Thus, (a), (b) and (c) are true in the initial configuration.

For the inductive step, assume the properties are true in any configuration C of the execution. We will show they are true in the following configuration C'.

Case 1: Suppose between the two configurations, node i executes lines 1–3. By assumption on the execution, i is not active in C, and by definition, i is active in C'. By the inductive hypothesis (b), $succ_i = \perp$ and $parent_i \neq i$ in C. By the code, $parent_i = i$ and $enq(i)$ is in transit in C'.

These changes do not affect the truth of (a), (b) and (c) for any node other than possibly i. In C', (a) is true for i because there is an $enq(i)$ message in transit. In C', (b) is true vacuously for i, since i is now active. In C', (c) is true for i by the code, since $succ_i$ is not changed (and was $\perp$ in C).

Case 2: Suppose between the two configurations, node i executes lines 4–8, i.e., i receives an $enq(k)$ message from node j. Then in C, $enq(k)$ is in transit. There is no change in the set of active nodes as a result of this event. By the inductive hypothesis (b), k is active in C, and thus also in C'. By the code, $parent_i = j$ in C', and either $succ_i = k$ or $enq(k)$ is in transit in C', depending on whether i is a sink in C.

By the code, (a) remains true for active node k. The only way that (a) could be invalidated for any other active node is if $succ_i$ holds the id of another node in C and this value is overwritten by k in C'. But $succ_i$ is overwritten only if $parent_i = i$ in C, and by the inductive hypothesis (c), $succ_i = \perp$ in C.

None of the changes made can affect the validity of (b).

The only change that can affect the validity of (c) is if $succ_i$ is set to a non-$\perp$ value. But in this case, $parent_i$ is set to something other than i, so (c) is vacuous for i. ∎

For active node i, define A_i to be the subset of A consisting of the set of nodes $\{i\} \cup \{j \in A : i < j \text{ or } j < i\}$. Note that for distinct i and j, either $A_i = A_j$ or $A_i \cap A_j = \emptyset$.

Lemma 6.2   *In every configuration of the execution, $(A, <)$ is a collection of total orders, i.e., for each $i \in A$, $(A_i, <)$ is a total order.*

Proof. The proof is by induction on the configurations. The basis follows since $A = \{r_0\}$ in the initial configuration.

For the inductive step, suppose the lemma is true in configuration C of the execution. We show it is true in the next configuration C'. The relation is changed only if line 6 is executed. In this case, since $enq(k)$ is in transit in C, Lemma 6.1(a) implies that no node has $succ$ equal to k. Thus, since by the inductive hypothesis, A_k is a total order in C, k is the head of $(A_k, <)$. Since the precondition for executing line 6 is that $parent_i = i$, it follows from Lemma 6.1(c) that $succ_i = \perp$.

Thus, since by the inductive hypothesis, A_i is a total order in C, i is the tail of A_i. Finally, in C', the previous A_i and A_k are joined into a single total order, as $succ_i$ is set equal to k.   ∎

Lemma 6.3   *In every configuration of the execution, for each node i, if $r_0 \notin A_i$, then there is an $enq(h)$ message in transit, where h is the head of $(A_i, <)$.*

Proof. The proof is by induction on the configurations. The basis follows since $A = \{r_0\}$ in the initial configuration.

For the inductive step, suppose the lemma is true in configuration C of the execution. We show it is true in the next configuration C'.

Case 1: Suppose between the two configurations, node i executes lines 1–3. By assumption on the execution, i is inactive in C, and thus does not appear in the relation. The effect of this event is to make a singleton in the relation, i.e., $A_i = \{i\}$, i is at the head, and $enq(i)$ is in transit.

Case 2: Suppose between the two configurations, node i executes lines 4–8, i.e., i receives an $enq(k)$ message from node j.

Case 2.1: Suppose $parent_i \neq i$ in C. Then $enq(k)$ is forwarded. There is no change to the relation, and there is still an enq in transit. The inductive hypothesis for C implies correctness for C'.

Case 2.2: Suppose $parent_i = i$ in C. By Lemma 6.1(b)(iv), i is active in C. By the inductive hypothesis, if A_i does not contain r_0 in C, then there is an $enq(h)$ message in transit in C, where h is the head of $(A_i, <)$. In C', $succ_i$ is set equal to k. As a result, $(A_k, <)$ is appended to the end of $(A_i, <)$, and in C', A_k is the same as A_i and the head of $(A_i, <)$ is still h. Thus, the lemma is true for i and for k.   ∎

The next Lemma states that when an enq message is in transit between two nodes, those two nodes are not each other's parents (cf. the dotted edges in Figures 6.1 and 6.2). It also states that there are no two-cycles in the orientation of the spanning tree induced by the *parent* variables.

Lemma 6.4   *Consider any configuration of the execution and any two neighboring nodes j and k.*

(a) *If $enq(i)$ is in transit from j to k for any node i, then $parent_j \neq k$ and $parent_k \neq j$.*

(b) *If $parent_j = k$, then $parent_k \neq j$.*

Proof. The proof is by induction on the configurations. The basis for (a) follows since no messages are in transit in the initial configuration. The basis for (b) follows by the assumed initialization of the *parent* variables.

For the inductive step, suppose the lemma is true in configuration C of the execution. We show it is true in the next configuration C'.

Case 1: Suppose between the two configurations, some node i executes lines 1–3. [[By the assumption that each node experiences at most one queueing request, i is inactive in C, and so by Lemma 6.1(b) (iv), $parent_i \neq i$ in C.]] Suppose $parent_i = j$ in C. By inductive hypothesis (b), $parent_j \neq i$ in C. During this event, $enq(i)$ is sent from i to j and i's parent is changed to be i itself. Thus, (a) is true in C'. These changes do not affect the validity of (b), so it is still true in C'.

Case 2: Suppose between the two configurations, some node i executes lines 4–8, i.e., i receives an $enq(k)$ message from node j. By the code, i changes its parent to j in C'. We now argue that this does not violate (b). In C, since an enq message is in transit from j to i, $parent_j \neq i$ by inductive hypothesis (a). Since j's local state does not change in going from C to C', it is still the case that $parent_j \neq i$.

The validity of (a) is only possibly affected if i forwards $enq(k)$ in C'. By the code, i sends this message to its old parent, h. By inductive hypothesis (a), since in C an enq message is in transit from j to i, it follows that h, i's old parent, is not equal to j in C. In C', i's parent has changed to be j, i.e., i's parent is not h. By inductive hypothesis (b), since h is i's old parent, i is not h's old parent in C, and, since no changes are made to h's local state in going from C to C', it remains true in C' that i is not h's parent. Thus, (a) is true in C with respect to the newly forwarded enq message. ■

The previous lemma implies that, for every active node i, as $enq(i)$ is forwarded through the spanning tree, it can never turn around: when it is received by node k from node j, if it is forwarded, it must be forwarded to some neighbor of k other than j. Thus, it must eventually hit some kind of endpoint and no longer be forwarded. Once it is no longer forwarded, Lemma 6.3 tells us that A_i now includes r_0. This, together with Lemma 6.2, gives us:

Theorem 6.5   There exists a configuration in the execution after which the relation $(A, <)$ never changes and it is a (single) total order.

6.3   DISCUSSION

In the last section, we proved the correctness of the Arrow protocol under some simplifying assumptions: each process makes at most one queueing request, the graph is static, and there are no failures. Several other aspects of the behavior of the protocol have been addressed in the literature, some of which we summarize next.

Building on work in [25, 27], Herlihy et al. [23] analyzed the cost of the Arrow protocol when communication is asynchronous and nodes can initiate requests at arbitrary times. The cost measure of interest is the sum, over all requests, of the time that elapses between when the request is initiated and when a node learns that this request is its successor. In the asynchronous model, time is measured by assuming that each message has a delay of at most one time unit. Herlihy et al. used a competitive analysis, which compares the cost of the Arrow protocol to the cost of an ideal algorithm. The ideal algorithm has two important advantages over Arrow: first, it has initial knowledge of all the requests that will occur, and second, it can communicate over any edge in the graph, instead of only over the spanning tree. As a result of the second advantage, for instance, communication can take place over shortest paths. Let s, the *stretch* of the spanning tree T used by Arrow, be the maximum, over all pairs of vertices u and v, of the ratio of the distance between u and v in T and the distance between u and v in G. Let D be the diameter of T. Then for any set of requests, the ratio of the cost of Arrow to the cost of the ideal algorithm is $O(s \cdot \log D)$. An almost-matching lower bound on this ratio is also proved.

Herlihy and Tirthapura [24] presented a fault-tolerant version of the Arrow protocol with local self-stabilizing actions. A system is *self-stabilizing* if, starting from an arbitrary initial global state, it eventually reaches a "legal" global state and remains in a legal state from thereon. They show that the time needed to self-stabilize the Arrow protocol from an arbitrary global state is constant, using only local actions, by decomposing the global predicate defining legality into the conjunction of local predicates, one for each edge of the spanning tree.

CHAPTER 7

Scheduling in a Graph

In this section, we present some theoretical results regarding the behavior of FR in graphs where there is no destination, that is, every node tries to avoid being a sink. The result, as will be shown, is that every node is a sink infinitely often. The primary application is in scheduling, where every node should be scheduled to take some action infinitely often (say, when it is a sink), while still satisfying some exclusion properties, such as no neighboring nodes are scheduled simultaneously. In the next section we present the Chandy and Misra distributed resource allocation algorithm [7], which uses these link reversal ideas.

In Section 7.1 we present the modified FR algorithm, give some necessary definitions, and prove some preliminary facts about the algorithm's behavior. The next two subsections focus on analyzing the "concurrency" of the algorithm, with the tree case covered in Section 7.2 and general graphs in Section 7.3. We conclude with a discussion in Section 7.4. This material is due to Barbosa and Gafni [2].

7.1   PRELIMINARIES

Suppose we reconsider the set-up in Sections 2 and 3 and dispense with the notion of a distinguished vertex in the graph (the destination). Recall that every vertex *other than the destination* that is a sink would reverse some links in that section, while the destination never did any reversals. Algorithm FRND, whose pseudocode is given as Algorithm 9, is FR in the absence of a destination. As we will analyze in detail, the result is an algorithm that never terminates: the number of sinks in the graph never decreases and in fact might increase, while the locations of the sinks continually change.

Algorithm 9: Full Reversal with No Destination (FRND)

    Input: directed graph $\vec{G} = (V, \vec{E})$

1 **while** $\vec{G}$ has a sink **do**

2   choose a nonempty subset S of sinks in $\vec{G}$

3   **foreach** $v \in S$ **do** reverse the direction of all links incident on v

4 **end**

Consider an input graph $\vec{G}$ that is an orientation of a connected undirected graph $G = (V, E)$ with no self-loops. First, we recall that Lemma 2.1 tells us that if a directed graph is acyclic, then it has at least one sink. Now we show that every iteration of FRND in the execution on $\vec{G}$ preserves acyclicity; the argument is the same as for FR, cf. Lemma 2.4. These two facts are used to show that every vertex is a sink infinitely often.

Lemma 7.1   *FRND maintains acyclicity.*

Theorem 7.2   In the execution of FRND on $\vec{G}$ every vertex is a sink infinitely often.

Proof.   By Lemma 7.1, FRND preserves acyclicity. Thus by Lemma 2.1, at each iteration of the algorithm, there is at least one sink. Thus FRND never terminates.

Since the number of vertices in $\vec{G}$ is finite, some vertex takes an infinite number of steps. Let W be the subset of vertices that take an infinite number of steps. Assume in contradiction that some vertex takes only a finite number of steps. Since G is connected, there exists an edge in G between a vertex u in W and a vertex v in $V - W$. Let t be the iteration of the while loop of FRND at which v takes its last step. Immediately after this iteration, the link between u and v is directed toward u. After u takes its first step subsequent to iteration t, the link becomes directed toward v. But since v takes no more steps, the link remains directed toward v forever afterwards, and u can take no more steps, contradiction.   ∎

Now we know that every vertex takes an infinite number of steps. This is good for resource allocation applications. It is now of interest to get a handle on how frequently vertices take steps with respect to each other. For this analysis, we focus solely on greedy executions, in which all sinks take a step at every iteration.

Consider the example in Figure 7.1. Note that initially there is just one sink, then there are two sinks, then three, until eventually every other vertex is a sink, and the set of sinks and non-sinks alternates in a repeating pattern. Note that executing PR on this graph gives very poor behavior: never more than one vertex is a sink at a time. (This provides some motivation for why we consider only FR where there is no destination.)

It turns out that this behavior is not a fluke. Every directed acyclic graph shows this kind of behavior: possibly an initial prefix of the execution that is not periodic, and then a repeating pattern.

Denote by $g(\vec{G})$ the directed graph resulting from executing one "greedy" iteration of FRND on $\vec{G}$, in which every sink takes a step. We will represent a greedy execution as the sequence of orientations before each iteration; note that the i-th orientation starting from initial orientation $\vec{G}_0$ is $g^{(i)}(\vec{G}_0)$.

Theorem 7.3   Every greedy execution of FRND starting from a connected directed acyclic graph is of the form $\alpha\beta\beta\beta\ldots$ where α is a (possibly empty) sequence of orientations and β is a (nonempty) sequence of orientations.

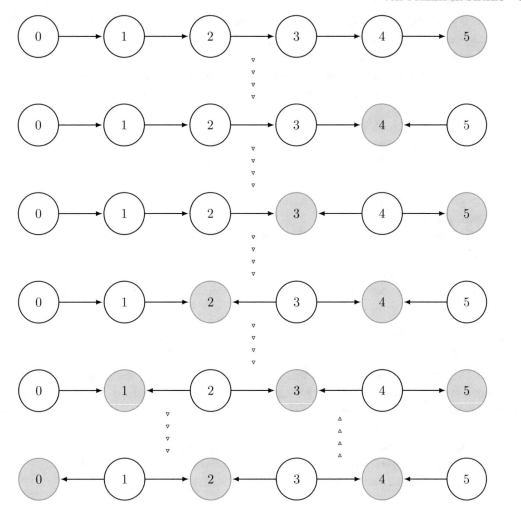

Figure 7.1: Execution of FRND starting with a path; the last two orientations are periodic with length 2 and multiplicity 1.

Proof. Consider a greedy execution $\vec{G}_0, \vec{G}_1, \vec{G}_2, \ldots$. For each $i \geq 0$, let S_i be the set of vertices in $\vec{G}_i$ that are sinks; since the execution is greedy, $\vec{G}_{i+1}$ is obtained from $\vec{G}_i$ by reversing all links incident on all vertices in S_i. Since the number of vertices in G is finite, there exist distinct i and j such that $S_i = S_j$. Note that if $S_i = S_j$, then $S_{i+1} = S_{j+1}$.

Let i and j be the smallest integers such that $i < j$ and $S_i = S_j$. By setting $\alpha = \vec{G}_0, \ldots, \vec{G}_{i-1}$ and $\beta = \vec{G}_i, \ldots, \vec{G}_{j-1}$, we fulfill the statement of the Theorem. ■

If β is of minimal length, then β is a *period* for $\vec{G}$, and every orientation in β is *periodic*. Note that every vertex appears at least once in a period, since every vertex takes steps infinitely often. We can proceed to analyze this behavior further.

(1) How long can it take until the execution becomes periodic? Malka and Rajsbaum [30] proved that the preperiodic part of an execution has length that is at most polynomial in the number of vertices.

(2) How long is the period? The period length must always be at least 2, since neighbors cannot be sinks simultaneously and the graph is connected. Malka et al. [29] proved that there are periodic orientations for which the period length is exponential in the number of vertices; in a specific family of graphs consisting of numerous circuits, with carefully chosen directions for the links, hooked together appropriately, it is shown that the period length is $e^{\Omega(\sqrt{n})}$, where e is the base of the natural logarithm.

(3) How "fair" is the period to different vertices? The bulk of this subsection is devoted to this question.

Let $W_v(t)$ be the number of steps taken by vertex v through iteration t. Let $dist_G(u, v)$ be the distance, in G, between vertices u and v (i.e., the number of edges in the shortest, undirected, path).

Lemma 7.4   *For any u and v in V, $|W_u(t) - W_v(t)| \leq dist_G(u, v)$.*

Proof. The proof is by induction on the distance. Suppose u and v are neighbors in G, so the distance between them is 1. Then, since the edge between them alternates direction every time u or v takes a step, we get that the number of steps taken by u and the number of steps taken by v never differ by more than 1 (cf. Lemma 3.11).

Suppose the Lemma is true for distance $d - 1$ and show for distance d. Let u and v be two vertices at distance d apart in G. Let x be a neighbor of v whose distance to u is $d - 1$; x must exist by properties of shortest paths. For any iteration t, we have:

$$
\begin{aligned}
|W_u(t) - W_v(t)| &= |(W_u(t) - W_x(t)) + (W_x(t) - W_v(t))| \\
&\leq |W_u(t) - W_x(t)| + |W_x(t) - W_v(t)| \\
&\leq (d - 1) + |W_x(t) - W_v(t)| \quad \text{by the inductive hypothesis} \\
&\leq (d - 1) + 1 \quad \text{by the same argument as in the base case} \\
&= d.
\end{aligned}
$$

∎

With the help of the previous Lemma, we can show in the next theorem that the periods are very fair.

Theorem 7.5   If β is a period for a graph G, then every vertex takes the same number of steps in β.

Proof.   Suppose in contradiction vertex u appears a times in β and another vertex v appears b times in β, with $b > a$. Consider the greedy execution consisting of β repeated infinitely often. For each $k \geq 1$, after the k-th copy of the period, u has taken $k \cdot a$ steps and v has taken $k \cdot b$ steps. Since k grows without bound, eventually $k \cdot b - k \cdot a$ exceeds $dist_G(u, v)$, which contradicts Lemma 7.4. ∎

This common value, the number of times that each vertex takes a step in a period, is called the *multiplicity* of the period. Consider a period of length p and multiplicity m. We define the *concurrency* of the period to be m/p. This quantity is the fraction of iterations during which any given vertex takes steps. Note that this quantity is also relevant to greedy executions that have a non-periodic prefix, as the contribution of the prefix gets smaller and smaller the longer the execution becomes. See Figure 7.2 for an example.

How big can the concurrency be? Suppose it is more than 1/2. Then for two neighboring vertices i and j, i takes steps more than half the time and j takes steps more than half the time. So at least some of the time, i and j are taking steps simultaneously, which is a contradiction, since vertices only take steps when they are sinks.

How small can the concurrency be? Not worse than $1/|V| = 1/n$, since at least one vertex takes a step at each iteration. (This would be the case when vertices take steps one at a time)

We now derive an exact expression for the concurrency of an orientation, which is a function of certain properties of the input graph. The analysis is facilitated by the concept of "rank" and some basic properties about rank. Given an orientation $\vec{G}$, define the *rank* of a vertex v, to be the length of the longest directed path from v to a sink; the rank of a sink is 0.

Lemma 7.6   *If (u, v) is a link in an orientation, then the rank of u must be larger than the rank of v.*

Proof.   Suppose the rank of u is r_u and the rank of v is r_v. Let π be a path of length r_v from v to a sink. Then there is a path of length $r_v + 1$ from u to a sink: take the link (u, v) and then follow π. Thus, r_u must be at least $r_v + 1$. ∎

Lemma 7.7   *Consider any orientation $\vec{G}$ and any vertex v in $\vec{G}$. If the rank of v is i in $\vec{G}$, where $i \geq 1$, then the rank of v in $g(\vec{G})$ is $i - 1$. If the rank of v is 0 in $\vec{G}$, then the rank of v in $g(\vec{G})$ is the maximum rank over all neighbors of v in $\vec{G}$.*

Proof.   For the case when $i \geq 1$, the proof is by strong induction on i. For the basis, suppose the rank of v in $\vec{G}$ is 1. Then every outgoing neighbor of v is a sink in $\vec{G}$, and in $g(\vec{G})$, v is a sink, with rank 0. Suppose the claim is true for all values of the rank from 1 to $i - 1$. Consider a vertex v with rank i in $\vec{G}$. Every outgoing neighbor of v has rank at most $i - 1$ and at least one has rank equal to $i - 1$. By induction, every outgoing neighbor of v with rank at least 1 reduces its rank by 1 in $g(\vec{G})$ and remains an outgoing neighbor of v. Every outgoing neighbor of v with rank 0 does a reversal,

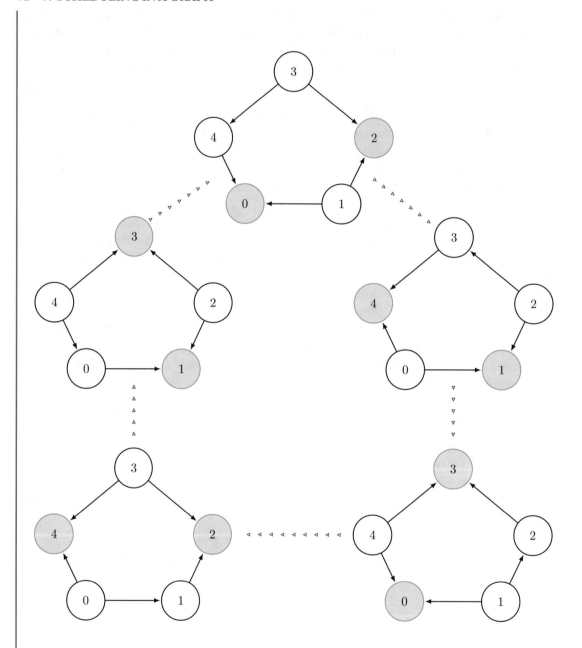

Figure 7.2: Execution of FRND on a 5-vertex ring. Period length is 5, multiplicity is 2, and concurrency is 2/5.

and thus there is no path from v that goes through such a neighbor in $g(\vec{G})$. Therefore in $g(\vec{G})$, the longest path from v to a sink goes through one of the outgoing neighbors with (new) rank $i - 2$, and the rank of v becomes $i - 1$.

Now consider the case when $i = 0$. Every neighbor of v is incoming in $\vec{G}$ and thus has a rank at least 1. Let u be a neighbor of v with largest rank in $\vec{G}$, say r. In $g(\vec{G})$, all the neighbors of v are now outgoing and, by the first part of the lemma, each neighbor of v reduces its rank by 1. Thus, a longest path from v to a sink goes through u and the rank of v is r. ∎

7.2   ANALYSIS FOR TREES

First, let's consider the case of trees. We'll show that no matter what the starting orientation, eventually the greedy execution becomes periodic with length 2 and multiplicity 1, for an optimal concurrency of 1/2.

Lemma 7.8   *For every tree G, starting with any orientation of G, the greedy execution of FRND eventually reaches an orientation in which every vertex has rank either 0 or 1.*

Proof. It follows from Lemma 7.7 that if the largest rank in an orientation is r, then in every subsequent orientation of the greedy execution, the maximum rank is at most r.

Suppose, in contradiction to the statement of the lemma, that there is a greedy execution of FRND on an orientation of a tree that has a suffix such that in every orientation of the suffix, the maximum rank is always r, for some value of r that is larger than 1.

In each orientation of the suffix, there must be a vertex u with rank r that is a neighbor of a sink v; in the following orientation, v takes on rank r and u's rank becomes $r - 1$. In at least one such situation, the vertex v must have another neighbor x that is a sink; otherwise the rank r would "die out" at this point, as it would not be adopted by any neighbor of v and v's rank would reduce to $r - 1$. Since $r \geq 2$, this sink neighbor x cannot be vertex u, since u has rank $r - 1 > 0$. Thus the rank r keeps "moving" away from its "original" location. Since G is a tree, eventually we hit a leaf; that is, v is a leaf and has no neighbor other than u, the node from which it adopted r. So every instance of r, including new ones that can be created by copying, eventually dies out; see Figure 7.3. ∎

Theorem 7.9   If G is a tree, then starting with any orientation of G, the greedy execution of FRND eventually reaches a periodic orientation with length 2 and multiplicity 1.

Proof. By Lemma 7.8, eventually an orientation is reached in which the only ranks are 0 and 1. By Lemma 7.7, in the next orientation, the ranks reverse. Thus we have a period with length 2 and multiplicity 1. ∎

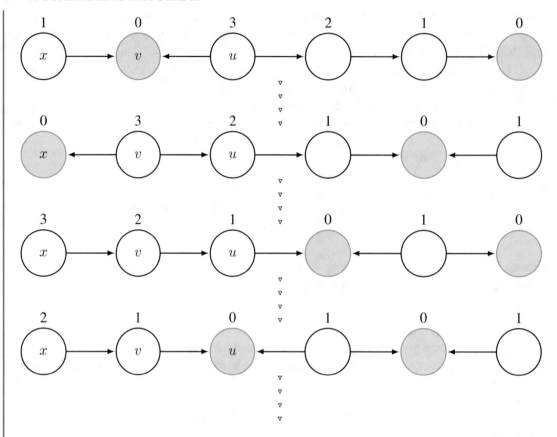

Figure 7.3: Tree example: rank 3 moves left from u to v to leaf x and then disappears.

Corollary 7.10   *For every tree G and every periodic orientation $\vec{G}$ of G, the concurrency of the greedy FRND execution on $\vec{G}$ is 1/2.*

7.3   ANALYSIS FOR NON-TREES

Now we consider graphs that are not trees. Given an orientation $\vec{G}$ of a graph that is not a tree, let $K(\vec{G})$ be the set of all circuits in $\vec{G}$. For a circuit $\vec{\kappa}$, let $|\kappa|$ be the number of vertices in the circuit and $r(\vec{\kappa})$ be the number of right-way links in the circuit. We will show that the concurrency of a periodic orientation, which is defined as the multiplicity m divided by the length of the period p, is a simple function of properties of circuits in the orientation. In particular, we will show that the concurrency of a periodic orientation $\vec{G}$ is the minimum, over all circuits $\vec{\kappa}$ in $K(\vec{G})$, of the ratio

$r(\vec{\kappa})/|\kappa|$. We first show, in Theorem 7.11, that for every circuit this ratio is at least m/p. Then we show, in Theorem 7.15, that there exists a circuit for which this ratio is at most m/p.

Theorem 7.11   For every graph G that is not a tree, every periodic orientation $\vec{G}$ of G with period length p and multiplicity m, and every circuit $\vec{\kappa}$ in $\vec{G}$,

$$\frac{r(\vec{\kappa})}{|\kappa|} \geq \frac{m}{p}.$$

Proof.   Let $\vec{G}_0, \vec{G}_1, \ldots, \vec{G}_{p-1}$ be the period starting with $\vec{G} = \vec{G}$. Let $\vec{\kappa}_i$ be the orientation of κ in $\vec{G}_i$, $0 \leq i < p$.

Observation 1: For all i and j, $0 \leq i, j < p$, $r(\vec{\kappa}_i) = r(\vec{\kappa}_j)$. The reason is that the value of r for every circuit is invariant throughout the execution of FRND: a sink in the circuit becomes a source in the circuit and the number of right-way links stays the same. Thus the sum, over all p orientations of the circuit in the period, of $r(\vec{\kappa}_i)$ is p times $r(\vec{\kappa})$.

Observation 2: For each i, $0 \leq i < p$, $r(\vec{\kappa}_i)$ is at least as large as $S(\vec{\kappa}_i)$, the number of sinks in $\vec{G}_i$ that are in the circuit $\vec{\kappa}_i$. The reason is that each such sink contributes 1 to the number of right-way links.

So we have:

$$
\begin{aligned}
\frac{r(\vec{\kappa})}{|\kappa|} &= \frac{1}{|\kappa|} \cdot \frac{1}{p} \cdot \sum_{i=0}^{p-1} r(\vec{\kappa}_i) && \text{by Observation 1} \\
&\geq \frac{1}{|\kappa|} \cdot \frac{1}{p} \cdot \sum_{i=0}^{p-1} S(\vec{\kappa}_i) && \text{by Observation 2} \\
&\geq \frac{1}{|\kappa|} \cdot \frac{1}{p} \cdot m \cdot |\kappa| && \text{since each of the } |\kappa| \text{ vertices in } \kappa \\
& && \text{is a sink } m \text{ times during the period} \\
&= \frac{m}{p}.
\end{aligned}
$$

■

For showing the upper bound on the ratio, we start as a warm-up by considering the special case when the multiplicity of the period is 1. Before proceeding, we need more knowledge about the behavior of rank in this case.

Lemma 7.12   *Consider a period with length p and multiplicity 1. In every orientation of the period, the maximum rank is $p - 1$ and each sink has at least one neighbor with rank $p - 1$.*

Proof. Let $\vec{G}_0, \ldots, \vec{G}_{p-1}$ be the period. Lemma 7.7 states that the rank of a vertex decreases by one in each subsequent orientation of the period until reaching 0. So vertices with rank i in $\vec{G}_0$ are sinks in $\vec{G}_i, 0 \leq i < p$. Since every vertex is a sink at least once in the period, the maximum rank cannot be more than $p - 1$. And since every vertex is a sink at most once in the period, the rank of any vertex v that is a sink in $\vec{G}_0$ must be at least $p - 1$ in $\vec{G}_1$, and so, by Lemma 7.7, v must have a neighbor whose rank in $\vec{G}_0$ is at least $p - 1$. $\blacksquare$

Theorem 7.13   For every graph G that is not a tree and every periodic orientation $\vec{G}$ of G with period length p and multiplicity 1, there exists a circuit $\vec{\kappa}$ in $K(\vec{G})$ such that

$$\frac{r(\vec{\kappa})}{|\kappa|} \leq \frac{1}{p}.$$

Proof. Suppose $p = 2$. Consider any circuit $\vec{\kappa}$ in $\vec{G}$. By Lemma 7.6, the circuit must consist of an even number of vertices, with ranks alternating between 0 and 1. So the directions of the links in the circuits alternate. Thus, $r(\vec{\kappa})/|\kappa| = 1/2 = 1/p$.

Now suppose $p \geq 3$. We will construct a circuit $\vec{\kappa}$ in $\vec{G}$ as follows. Let s_0 be any sink. By Lemma 7.12, s_0 has a neighbor v_1 with rank $p - 1$. By definition of rank, there is a path from v_1 to a sink s_1 of length $p - 1$, and the ranks of the vertices along this path are $p - 1, p - 2, \ldots, 2, 1, 0$. If $s_1 = s_0$, then we have a circuit.

If $s_1 \neq s_0$, then we apply the same argument again: By Lemma 7.12, s_1 has a neighbor v_2 with rank $p - 1$ and there is a path from v_1 to a sink s_2 of length $p - 1$, and the ranks of the vertices along this path are $p - 1, p - 2, \ldots, 2, 1, 0$. If s_2 equals either s_0 or s_1, then we have a circuit.

We continue in this fashion. Eventually, the sink at the end of the path must be the same as one of the previously encountered sinks, since the graph is finite, and we have a circuit.

Let $\vec{\kappa}$ be the *reverse* of the circuit just constructed. It consists of q segments, each segment being a sequence of vertices with increasing rank $(0, 1, 2, \ldots, p - 1)$, followed by the first vertex. All the links in each segment are wrong-way, since they correspond to the reverse of the paths from the construction. All the links that go between segments (from a vertex with rank $p - 1$ to a sink) are right-way. The length of $\vec{\kappa}$ is $q \cdot p$ and the number of right-way links is q (one per segment). Thus $r(\vec{\kappa})/|\kappa| = q/(qp) = 1/p$. $\blacksquare$

It remains to deal with the case when $m > 1$. For this, we relate the problem to a coloring problem.

An *m-tuple p-coloring* (or *multi-coloring*) of an orientation $\vec{G} = (V, \vec{E})$ assigns a tuple of m distinct increasing integers (or "colors") to each vertex in V, where each integer is between 0 and $p - 1$ inclusive. An m-tuple p-coloring is said to be *interleaved* if for each link $(v, u) \in \vec{E}$, the colors in u's tuple are interleaved with the colors in v's tuple, starting with u's smallest. More formally, if u's tuple is $(c_1, c_2, \ldots, c_m)$ and v's tuple is $(d_1, d_2, \ldots, d_m)$, then $c_1 < d_1 < c_2 < d_2 < \ldots < c_m < d_m$.

An m-tuple p-coloring is said to be *smooth* if, for each color c, every node in V whose tuple includes color c has a neighbor (either incoming or outgoing) whose tuple includes color $(c - 1) \mod p$.

Barbosa and Gafni [2] prove the following correspondence between periodic orientations and multi-colorings that are interleaved and smooth. The reason for introducing the coloring is explained just after the next Theorem.

Theorem 7.14   Let $\vec{G}$ be an orientation. $\vec{G}$ is periodic with period length p and multiplicity m if and only if $\vec{G}$ has an m-tuple p-coloring that is interleaved and smooth.

Proof. We just sketch the main ideas; see [2] for details.

Suppose $\vec{G}$ is periodic with length p and multiplicity m. Color each vertex with the tuple that tells at which orientations of the period the vertex is a sink. For example, if $\vec{G}$ is the top orientation in Figure 7.2, then node 2 is colored with the tuple (0,3) since 2 is a sink in the 0-th and the 3rd orientations of the period starting with $\vec{G}$. Since $\vec{G}$ has period p, every tuple element is between 0 and $p - 1$, and since $\vec{G}$ has multiplicity m, every tuple has m elements. The multi-coloring is interleaved because neighbors take turns being sinks, starting with the vertex with the incoming link. To show that the multi-coloring is smooth, note that each vertex that is a sink in one of the orientations of a period must have a neighbor that is a sink in the preceding orientation.

For the other direction, assume $\vec{G}$ has an m-tuple p-coloring that is interleaved and smooth. For each $i, 0 \leq i < p$, let $\vec{G}_i = g^{(i)}(\vec{G})$. We will show that this sequence of orientations is a period, i.e., we will show there are no repeats in the sequence, and that one more iteration brings us back to $\vec{G}_0 = \vec{G}$. We first note that every vertex with 0 in its tuple is a sink in $\vec{G}$; this is true by the interleaved assumption. We then note that every sink has 0 in its tuple; this follows from the smoothness assumption. Thus the set of vertices that are sinks in $\vec{G} = \vec{G}_0$ are exactly those with 0 in their color tuple. Barbosa and Gafni [2] then continue this argument inductively to show that, for each c between 1 and $p - 1$, the set of nodes that are sinks in $\vec{G}_c$ is exactly the set of nodes that have c in their tuple.   ∎

We now explain the usefulness of the previous theorem. To show that any periodic orientation $\vec{G}$ with length p and multiplicity m has a circuit with the desired property, we construct another graph $\vec{G}^*$ based on the original graph. We use one direction of the previous theorem to deduce that there is an m-tuple p-coloring of the original graph $\vec{G}$. We use this coloring to construct a 1-tuple p-coloring of the new graph $\vec{G}^*$, and then use the other direction of the previous theorem to deduce that $\vec{G}^*$ has period p and multiplicity 1. Since $\vec{G}^*$ has multiplicity 1, we can use the proof of Theorem 7.13, which is only valid for the multiplicity 1 case, to obtain a circuit in $\vec{G}^*$ with a particular structure. Finally, we show that the projection of this circuit onto the original graph has the desired property.

Theorem 7.15   For every graph G that is not a tree and every periodic orientation $\vec{G}$ of G with period length p and multiplicity m, there exists a circuit κ in $K(G)$ such that

$$\frac{r(\vec{\kappa})}{|\kappa|} \leq \frac{m}{p}.$$

Proof. Suppose $\vec{G} = (V, \vec{E})$. Let $\vec{G}^*$ be the directed graph consisting of m copies of $\vec{G}$, with some additional links between vertices in different copies. Denote the set of vertices in the i-th copy of $\vec{G}$ by V^i, $0 \leq i < m$, and denote the copy of vertex $v \in V$ that is in V^i by v^i. Add an edge from v^i to u^j if and only if $i > j$ and either $u = v$ or $(u, v) \in \vec{E}$ or $(v, u) \in \vec{E}$. See Figure 7.4 for an example.

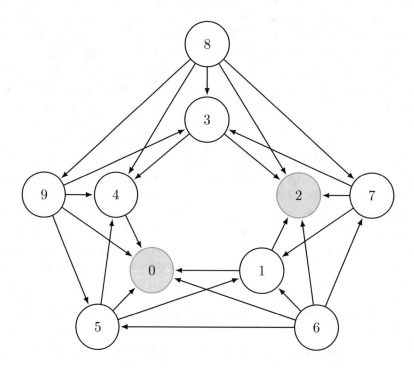

Figure 7.4: Graph resulting from transformation of 5-vertex ring in which 0 and 2 are sinks; vertex 5 is a copy of 0, 6 is a copy of 1, etc. Transformed graph has period length 5 and multiplicity 1.

Claim: $\vec{G}^*$ is periodic with period length p and multiplicity 1.
Proof of claim: See [2].

Theorem 7.13 states that there is a circuit $\vec{\kappa}^*$ in $\vec{G}^*$ such that $r(\vec{\kappa}^*)/|\kappa^*| \leq 1/p$. Looking into the proof of the theorem, we see that $\vec{\kappa}^*$ consists of some number, say q, of segments and in each segment the ranks of the vertices increase consecutively from 0 to $p - 1$. By definition of rank, all links within a segment are wrong-way, since a vertex with lower rank cannot have an outgoing neighbor with higher rank. Thus, the only possible right-way links are between segments.

Since all links within a segment are wrong-way, the segment must consist of a sequence of subsegments of vertices such that (1) within each subsegment, all vertices are in the same copy of $\vec{G}$, and (2) the copies corresponding to the subsegments have increasing indices. The reason is that the definition of $\vec{G}^*$ requires that links between difference vertices in different copies of $\vec{G}$ are directed from higher index to lower index. Since there are only m copies of $\vec{G}$ in $\vec{G}^*$, there can be at most m subsegments in each segment.

Let $\vec{\kappa}$ be the projection of $\vec{\kappa}^*$ onto $\vec{G}$, i.e., each vertex v^i in $\vec{\kappa}^*$ is replaced with v (the vertex that v^i is a copy of). The length of the circuit is not changed, i.e., $|\kappa| = qp$. We now show that there are at most m right-way links per segment, i.e., $r(\vec{\kappa}) \leq qm$, which will imply that the ratio is at most m/p, as desired. For each segment, the only links that can be right-way are those that go between two consecutive subsegments and the one at the end that goes to the next segment (recall that the last segment wraps around to first). As argued above, there are at most m such links. ∎

Theorems 7.11 and 7.15 together imply:

Corollary 7.16 *For every graph G that is not a tree and every periodic orientation $\vec{G}$ of G, the concurrency of the FRND execution on $\vec{G}$ is*

$$\min_{\vec{\kappa} \in K(\vec{G})} \left(\frac{r(\vec{\kappa})}{|\kappa|} \right).$$

Barbosa and Gafni [2] proved that it is actually sufficient to consider only simple cycles.

7.4   DISCUSSION

How can we choose an orientation for a graph that has the best concurrency? For trees, as we showed in Section 7.2, the initial orientation makes no difference, as eventually a periodic orientation with concurrency 1/2 is reached. However, for graphs that are not trees, it can make a huge difference: Consider a ring of n vertices that initially has a single sink. The location of the sink will rotate around the ring, but there will never be more than one sink. Thus, the concurrency is $1/n$, which is very poor. A better initial orientation is to have every other vertex be a sink (for even n), giving concurrency of 1/2. However, Barbosa and Gafni [2] proved that determining an initial orientation that gives the best concurrency is an NP-complete problem. To show the problem is NP-hard, they exploit the equivalence between having a particular concurrency and having a multi-coloring, they rephrase the optimization problem as a decision problem, and they reduce the classical coloring problem to the multi-coloring problem. The most complicated part is showing the problem is in NP.

FRND can be used to solve the "1-scheduling problem": think of the sinks as being scheduled, or allowed, to take some special action (such as use a resource or take a step of a simulated algorithm).

Since two neighbors cannot be sinks simultaneously, no vertex in the 1-neighborhood of a scheduled vertex is also scheduled. Malka et al. [29] studied a generalization of the 1-scheduling problem, called the d-scheduling problem for any integer $d \geq 1$, in which no vertex in the d-neighborhood of a scheduled vertex is also scheduled. The 2-scheduling problem captures the problem of scheduling nodes in a wireless network to broadcast without causing collisions. The d-scheduling problem can be reduced to the 1-scheduling problem by adding in extra links.

CHAPTER 8

Resource Allocation in a Distributed System

A well-known problem in distributed systems is the *dining philosophers problem*. It is a generalization of the mutual exclusion problem defined in Section 5.1. There is an arbitrary connected undirected graph, called the *conflict graph*, whose vertices correspond to the nodes; there is an edge between vertex i and j if nodes i and j compete for exclusive access to a resource. This problem models a situation where there are multiple resources, each resource can be used by only node at a time, different resources can be used at the same time, and each node may need multiple resources—corresponding to all its edges—to enter its critical section.

We assume that the topology of the conflict graph is a subset of the communication topology of the system. Analogously to the mutual exclusion problem, each node has a dining philosophers process and an application process that cooperate so that the application process cycles among remainder, waiting, and critical local states. The combination of the individual dining philosophers processes forms a distributed dining philosophers algorithm. A dining philosophers algorithm must ensure, for every execution:

Exclusion Condition: If any process is in its critical section, then no neighbor of the process in the conflict graph is in its critical section.

Fairness Condition: Every process requesting access to the critical section eventually enters the critical section.

One idea for solving the dining philosophers problem is to run the algorithm FRND from Section 7, and whenever a node is a sink, it can enter its critical section. By the behavior of FRND, each node will be a sink infinitely often and two neighboring nodes will never be sinks simultaneously. However, issues similar to those discussed in Section 4.1 arise in attempting to apply FRND in a system in which nodes communicate through asynchronous message passing (e.g., how do two neighboring nodes know which way the link between them should be directed?).

Chandy and Misra [7] developed an algorithm for the dining philosophers problem that uses link reversal ideas but handles asynchronous message passing. An important difference from FRND is that Chandy and Misra allow some nodes to stop participating in the competition for arbitrary periods of time, even permanently, in which case these nodes should not have to do any work on behalf of the nodes that are still contending for resources. In Section 8.1, we present the algorithm, adapted to the conventions in this monograph[1]. A correctness proof is sketched in Section 8.2.

8.1 CHANDY AND MISRA'S ALGORITHM

A key data structure in the algorithm is the *precedence graph*, which is a directed version of the conflict graph. The precedence graph is represented in a distributed fashion by having each node i keep a boolean variable $yieldTo_i[j]$ for each of its neighbors j. Informally speaking, the variable is true if and only if j has precedence over i. If the variable is true, consider the link to be directed from i to j. The $yieldTo$ variables are initialized so that the precedence graph is acyclic initially.

Each pair of neighboring nodes i and j share a single token, which ensures exclusive access to the resource shared by these two nodes. When i enters its waiting section, if it does not have the token shared with j, then it sends a request message to j.

The recipient j of a request message satisfies the request if it is not interested in accessing the shared resource, regardless of the precedence graph. However, if j is also waiting to enter the critical section, then the token is sent only if i has precedence over j, as indicated by j's variable $yieldTo_j[i]$. Thus the precedence graph is used to arbitrate between contending neighbors, but otherwise it is ignored. Whenever the token is sent from j to i, the link in the precedence graph is made incoming to i by having j set its $yieldTo_j[i]$ variable to false.

Once i has all the tokens for its shared resources, it enters the critical section. While it is in the critical section, any requests received are deferred. When i leaves the critical section, it updates the precedence graph using full reversal—it sets all its $yieldTo$ variables to true—and satisfies all deferred requests. By starting with an acyclic conflict graph and only modifying it through full reversal of sinks, the conflict graph remains acyclic, and thus there can be no deadlock caused by a cycle of nodes waiting on each other. When a deferred request is satisfied, meaning the shared token is sent, the precedence graph is updated so that the link between i and j is made incoming to i by setting $yieldTo_i[j]$ to false.

In more detail, each node i has the following local variables:

- $Neighbors_i$: static set of neighboring nodes in the topology

- $status_i$: REMAINDER, WAITING or CRITICAL

- $hasToken_i[j]$ for each $j \in Neighbors_i$: a boolean

- $yieldTo_i[j]$ for each $j \in Neighbors_i$: a boolean

- $pending_i$: a set of node ids

In the initial configuration C_0:

---

[1] The main changes are (1) the abandonment of the "eating" metaphor, and (2) the indication of j having precedence over i by considering the link to be directed from i to j instead of vice versa.

- $status_i =$ REMAINDER for all nodes i;

- $pending_i = \emptyset$, for all nodes i;

- For each pair of neighboring nodes i and j with $i < j$,

    - $hasToken_i[j] =$ true, $yieldTo_i[j] =$ true,
    - $hasToken_j[i] =$ false, $yieldTo_j[i] =$ false;

- no messages are in transit on any link.

See Figure 10 for the pseudocode.

8.2   CORRECTNESS OF CHANDY AND MISRA'S ALGORITHM

To analyze the behavior of the FRRA algorithm, we need the following definitions.

- For each unordered pair $\{i, j\}$ of neighboring nodes, each *Token* message in transit between i and j, in either direction, forms an $\{i, j\}$-*token*. Furthermore, if $hasToken_i[j]$, resp. $hasToken_j[i]$, is true, then we say that i, resp. j, has an $\{i, j\}$-*token*.

- For each unordered pair $\{i, j\}$ of neighboring nodes, each *Request* message in transit between i and j, in either direction, forms an $\{i, j\}$-*request*. Furthermore, if j is in $pending_i$, resp. i is in $pending_j$, then we say that i, resp. j, has an $\{i, j\}$-*request*.

In order to prove that the algorithm satisfies mutual exclusion, we use the fact, proved in the next lemma, that properties (a) and (b) are invariants. This fact is proved by induction on the execution, and relies on the fact that properties (c), (d), and (e) are invariants.

Lemma 8.1   *The following statements are true in every configuration of every execution. Let i and j be any pair of neighboring nodes.*

(a) *There is exactly one $\{i, j\}$-token.*

(b) *If $status_i =$ CRITICAL, then i has the $\{i, j\}$-token.*

(c) *If a Request message is in transit from i to j, then either a Token message precedes the Request message in the link to j, or j has the $\{i, j\}$-token.*

(d) *If a Request message is in transit from i to j, or if i is in $pending_j$, or if a Token message is in transit from j to i, then $status_i =$ WAITING.*

(e) *There is at most one $\{i, j\}$-request.*

Algorithm 10: Full Reversal Resource Allocation (FRRA) Algorithm (Chandy & Misra);
code for node i

---

1 **when** Application requests access to critical section (RequestCS):
2     $status :=$ WAITING
3   **if** *(hasToken[j] for each $j \in$ Neighbors)* **then**
4         $status :=$ CRITICAL (EnterCS)
5   **else foreach** j such that $\neg hasToken[j]$ **do** send *Request* message to j

6 **when** *Request* message received from node j:
7   **if** *yieldTo[j]* and *status* $\neq$ CRITICAL **then**
8   *hasToken[j]* := false
9   *yieldTo[j]* := false
10   send *Token* message to j
11   **if** *status* = WAITING **then** send *Request* message to j
12   **else** add j to *pending*

13 **when** *Token* message received from node j:
14   *hasToken[j]* := true
15   **if** *hasToken[k]* for each $k \in$ *Neighbors* **then**
16         $status :=$ CRITICAL (EnterCS)
17

18 **when** Application releases critical section (ReleaseCS):
19     $status :=$ REMAINDER
20   **foreach** $j \in$ *Neighbors* **do** *yieldTo[j]* := true
21   **foreach** $j \in$ *pending* **do**
22   *hasToken[j]* := false
23   *yieldTo[j]* := false
24   send *Token* message to j
25   **end**
26   *pending* := $\emptyset$

Theorem 8.2   Algorithm FRRA satisfies the exclusion condition (no two neighbors are critical simultaneously).

Proof. If node i is in the critical section, that is, $status_i =$ CRITICAL, then Lemma 8.1(b) states that i has the $\{i, j\}$-token for each of its neighbors j. By Lemma 8.1(a), neighbor j cannot have the $\{i, j\}$-token. Thus by Lemma 8.1(b), no neighbor of i is in the critical section, and exclusion is satisfied. ∎

The next set of invariants are needed to prove the fairness condition; they are proved by induction.

Lemma 8.3   *The following statements are true in every configuration of every execution. Let i and j be any pair of neighboring nodes.*

(a) *At least one of $yieldTo_i[j]$ and $yieldTo_j[i]$ is false.*

(b) *If a request message is in transit from i to j, or if j has the $\{i, j\}$-token or if a* Token *message is in transit from j to i, then $yieldTo_i[j] = false$.*

Given a configuration C_t of the algorithm, we define a directed graph $\vec{G}_t$, called the *precedence graph*, as follows. The vertices of $\vec{G}_t$ are the nodes, and the directed link (i, j) is in $\vec{G}_t$ if i and j are neighboring nodes and either (a) $yieldTo_i[j]$ is true and $yieldTo_j[i]$ is false, or (b) $yieldTo_i[j]$ and $yieldTo_j[i]$ are both false and either a *Token* message is in transit from i to j or $hasToken_j[i]$ is true. By Lemma 8.3(a), at least one of $yieldTo_i[j]$ and $yieldTo_j[i]$ is false. If only one of the variables is false, then the link between i and j in the precedence graph is directed toward the false one. If both variables are false, then the link is directed toward the node that has, or is about to have, the token. Thanks to Lemma 8.1(a), the direction of the link is uniquely defined.

The next lemma shows that the precedence graph is always acyclic. The main point in the proof is that when a node leaves the critical section, it becomes a source in the precedence graph, in effect executing a full reversal. Since a full reversal is the only way that the precedence graph changes, this behavior cannot cause a cycle. An important difference from FRND in Section 7 is that a node that is not a sink in the precedence graph can do a reversal: A node i can enter the critical section when it is not a sink in the precedence graph if some of its neighbors are not contending for the critical section, as the precedence graph is only used to arbitrate among contending nodes. Then when i leaves the critical section, it does a full reversal. This behavior is also different from that in the LRME mutex algorithm of Section 5.1.1, in which a non-sink node makes itself become a sink when it receives the token.

Lemma 8.4   *For each configuration C_t in the execution, $\vec{G}_t$ is acyclic.*

Proof.   The proof is by induction on the configurations in the execution. For the basis, the definition of the initial configuration ensures that $\vec{G}_0$ is acyclic, since (i, j) is in $\vec{G}_0$ if and only if i and j are neighbors and $i < j$. Since the node ids are totally ordered, there cannot be a cycle in $\vec{G}_0$.

For the inductive step, let C_{t-1} be the old configuration and C_t be the new one. By the inductive hypothesis, $\vec{G}_{t-1}$ is acyclic. We consider all events that can affect the precedence graph in C_t.

Case 1: When a *Request* message is received by i from j, it is possible that i changes $yieldTo_i[j]$ from true to false and sends a *Token* message to i. These changes keep the link between i and j directed from i to j in the precedence graph.

Case 2: When a *Token* message is received by i from j, the message is no longer in transit, but now j has the token. Thus if the link were directed from i to j in $\vec{G}_{t-1}$, it remains so in $\vec{G}_t$.

Case 3: Suppose the application at i finishes the critical section. By the code, in C_t, $yieldTo_i[j]$, for each j, is either true, or it is false but a *Token* message is in transit from i to j. Thus in $\vec{G}_t$, i is a source. Since $\vec{G}_{t-1}$ is acyclic, any cycle in $\vec{G}$ must involve node i, but since i has no incoming links, this is not possible.   ∎

Theorem 8.5   Algorithm FRRA satisfies the fairness condition (every waiting node eventually is critical).

Proof.   Suppose in contradiction, some nonempty set S of nodes are in their waiting section forever.

Let i be any member of S. Let t be the last time when i enters its waiting section. If i gives up a token to some neighbor j after t, then it sets $yieldTo_i[j]$ to false. If that token ever comes back to i after t, i will not subsequently give it up again, since the only way $yieldTo_i[j]$ can become true is for i to leave the critical section. Thus, eventually the set of tokens held by i stops changing. Note that the $yieldTo$ variables of node i also stop changing. As a result, the links in the precedence graph that are incident on nodes in S stop changing direction.

Consider a time after which the set of tokens held by every node in S does not change any more. Pick any node i_0 in S. Consider a neighbor i_1 of i_0 on which i_0 is waiting (i.e., i_0 does not have the $\{i_0, i_1\}$-token). Node i_1 must also be in S: otherwise, the next time that i_1 is in its REMAINDER* section, it will send the token to i_0, thanks to the *pending* set. Thus, it must be that i_1 has precedence over i_0, i.e., (i_0, i_1) is in the precedence graph.

Similarly, i_1 must be waiting on some neighbor i_2 that is also in S, where (i_1, i_2) is in the precedence graph. We continue this process until we have a path $(i, i_1, i_2, \ldots, i_m)$ in which there is some repeated node. This must happen since the graph is finite. But Lemma 8.4 shows that the precedence graph is always acyclic, a contradiction.   ∎

CHAPTER 9

Conclusion

In this monograph, we have presented a number of distributed algorithms that use the concept of link reversal. The algorithms considered have solved routing, leader election, mutual exclusion, distributed queueing, scheduling, and resource allocation. We have not attempted to provide a comprehensive survey of all the literature on these topics. In fact, this is not an exhaustive list of problems that have been tackled using link reversal; others include the k-mutual exclusion problem [41], the publish/subscribe problem [1, 14], implementing simulated annealing [3], coloring an anonymous planar graph [6], and simulating artificial neural network models [6]. Instead, we have focused in depth on a smaller number of fundamental papers to give a foundation on which the reader can build.

Perhaps one of the attractions of link reversal in distributed algorithms is that it provides a way for nodes in the system to observe their local neighborhoods, take only local actions, and yet cause global problems to be solved. We conjecture that future interesting uses of link reversal are yet to be discovered.

Bibliography

[1] E. Anceaume, A. K. Datta, M. Gradinariu, and G. Simon. Publish/subscribe scheme for mobile networks. In *Proceedings of the 2002 Workshop on Principles of Mobile Computing (POMC)*, pages 74–81, 2002. DOI: 10.1145/584490.584505 Cited on page(s) 87

[2] V. Barbosa and E. Gafni. Concurrency in heavily loaded neighborhood-constrained systems. *ACM Transactions on Programming Languages and Systems*, 11(4):562–584, 1989. DOI: 10.1145/69558.69560 Cited on page(s) 3, 67, 77, 78, 79

[3] V. Barbosa and E. Gafni. A distributed implementation of simulated annealing. *Journal of Parallel and Distributed Computing*, 6(2):411–434, 1989. DOI: 10.1145/777412.777446 Cited on page(s) 87

[4] C. Busch, S. Surapaneni, and S. Tirthapura. Analysis of link reversal routing algorithms for mobile ad hoc networks. In *Proceedings of the 15th ACM Symposium on Parallel Algorithms and Architectures (SPAA)*, pages 210–219, 2003. Cited on page(s) 1, 19, 20, 25, 29, 34

[5] C. Busch and S. Tirthapura. Analysis of link reversal routing algorithms. *SIAM Journal on Computing*, 35(2):305–326, 2005. DOI: 10.1137/S0097539704443598 Cited on page(s) 1, 19, 20, 25, 29, 34

[6] A. Calabrese and F. Franca. Distributed computing on neighbourhood constrained systems. In *Proceedings of the 3rd International Conference on Principles of Distributed Systems (OPODIS)*, pages 215–230, 1999. Cited on page(s) 87

[7] K. M. Chandy and J. Misra. The drinking philosophers problem. *ACM Transactions on Programming Languages and Systems*, 6(4):632–646, 1984. DOI: 10.1145/1780.1804 Cited on page(s) 3, 67, 81

[8] Y.-I. Chang, M. Singhal, and M. T. Liu. A fault tolerant algorithm for distributed mutual exclusion. In *9th IEEE Symposium on Reliable Distributed Systems*, pages 146–154, 1990. DOI: 10.1109/RELDIS.1990.93960 Cited on page(s) 56

[9] B. Charron-Bost, M. Függer, J. L. Welch, and J. Widder. Full reversal routing as a linear dynamical system. In *Proceedings of the 18th International Colloquium on Structural Information and Communication Complexity*, 2011. DOI: 10.1007/978-3-642-22212-2_10 Cited on page(s) 1, 29, 35

[10] B. Charron-Bost, M. Függer, J. L. Welch, and J. Widder. Partial is full. In *Proceedings of the 18th International Colloquium on Structural Information and Communication Complexity*, 2011. DOI: 10.1007/978-3-642-22212-2_11 Cited on page(s) 1, 29, 34, 35

[11] B. Charron-Bost, A. Gaillard, J. L. Welch, and J. Widder. Routing without ordering. In *Proceedings of the 21st ACM Symposium on Parallelism in Algorithms and Architectures (SPAA)*, pages 145–153, 2009. DOI: 10.1145/1583991.1584034 Cited on page(s) 1, 15, 17, 20, 21

[12] B. Charron-Bost, J. L. Welch, and J. Widder. Link reversal: How to play better to work less. In *Proceedings of the 5th International Workshop on Algorithmic Aspects of Wireless Sensor Networks*, 2009. DOI: 10.1007/978-3-642-05434-1_10 Cited on page(s) 1, 26, 28, 29

[13] A. Cornejo, S. Viqar, and J. L. Welch. Reliable neighbor discovery for mobile ad hoc networks. In *Proceedings of the DIALM-POMC Joint Workshop on Foundations of Mobile Computing*, pages 63–72, 2010. DOI: 10.1145/1860684.1860699 Cited on page(s) 38

[14] A. K. Datta, M. Gradinariu, M. Raynal, and G. Simon. Anonymous publish/subscribe in p2p networks. In *Proceedings of the 17th IEEE International Parallel and Distributed Processing Symposium (IPDPS)*, page 74, 2003. DOI: 10.1109/IPDPS.2003.1213174 Cited on page(s) 87

[15] M. J. Demmer and M. Herlihy. The arrow distributed directory protocol. In *Proceedings of the 12th International Symposium on Distributed Computing (DISC)*, pages 119–133, 1998. Cited on page(s) 2, 59

[16] D. Dhamdhere and S. Kulkarni. A token based k-resilient mutual exclusion algorithm for distributed systems. *Information Processing Letters*, 50(3):151–157, 1994. DOI: 10.1016/0020-0190(94)00019-0 Cited on page(s) 56

[17] E. W. Dijkstra. Hierarchical ordering of sequential processes. *Acta Informatica*, 1:115–138, 1971. DOI: 10.1007/BF00289519 Cited on page(s) 2

[18] C. Fetzer and F. Cristian. A highly available local leader election service. *IEEE Transactions on Software Engineering*, 25(5):603–618, 1999. DOI: 10.1109/32.815321 Cited on page(s) 44

[19] E. Gafni and D. Bertsekas. Distributed algorithms for generating loop-free routes in networks with frequently changing topology. *IEEE Transactions on Communications*, C-29(1):11–18, 1981. DOI: 10.1109/TCOM.1981.1094876 Cited on page(s) 1, 5, 8, 10, 12, 13, 14, 19, 38, 43

[20] A. Gaillard. *Problèmes de communication dans les systèmes distribués: ruptures et corruptions*. Ph.D. thesis, Ecole polytechnique, France, 2009. Cited on page(s) 20

[21] B. Heidergott, G. J. Olsder, and J. von der Woude. *Max plus at work*. Princeton Univ. Press, 2006. Cited on page(s) 31

[22] J.-M. Hélary, A. Mostéfaoui, and M. Raynal. A general scheme for token- and tree-based distributed mutual exclusion algorithms. *IEEE Transactions on Parallel and Distributed Systems*, 5(11):1185–1196, 1994. DOI: 10.1109/71.329670 Cited on page(s) 46

[23] M. Herlihy, F. Kuhn, S. Tirthapura, and R. Wattenhofer. Dynamic analysis of the arrow distributed protocol. *Theory of Computing Systems*, 39(6):875–901, 2006. DOI: 10.1007/s00224-006-1251-9 Cited on page(s) 2, 59, 65

[24] M. Herlihy and S. Tirthapura. Self-stabilizing distributed queuing. In *Proceedings of the 15th International Symposium on Distributed Computing (DISC)*, pages 209–223, 2001. DOI: 10.1109/TPDS.2006.94 Cited on page(s) 66

[25] M. Herlihy, S. Tirthapura, and R. Wattenhofer. Competitive concurrent distributed queuing. In *Proceedings of the 20th ACM Symposium on Principles of Distributed Computing (PODC)*, pages 127–133, 2001. DOI: 10.1145/383962.384001 Cited on page(s) 65

[26] R. Ingram, P. Shields, J. E. Walter, and J. L. Welch. An asynchronous leader election algorithm for dynamic networks. In *Proceedings of the 23rd IEEE International Parallel and Distributed Processing Symposium (IPDPS)*, pages 1–12, 2009. DOI: 10.1109/IPDPS.2009.5161028 Cited on page(s) 2, 43, 44

[27] F. Kuhn and R. Wattenhofer. Dynamic analysis of the arrow distributed protocol. In *Proceedings of the 16th ACM Symposium on Parallel Algorithms and Architectures (SPAA)*, pages 294–301, 2004. DOI: 10.1145/1007912.1007962 Cited on page(s) 65

[28] L. Lamport. Time, clocks and the ordering of events in a distributed system. *Communications of the ACM*, 21(7):558–565, 1978. DOI: 10.1145/359545.359563 Cited on page(s) 43

[29] Y. Malka, S. Moran, and S. Zaks. A lower bound on the period length of a distributed scheduler. *Algorithmica*, 10(5):383–398, 1993. DOI: 10.1007/BF01769705 Cited on page(s) 70, 80

[30] Y. Malka and S. Rajsbaum. Analysis of distributed algorithms based on recurrence relations (preliminary version). In *Proceedings of the 5th International Workshop on Distributed Algorithms (WDAG)*, pages 242–253, 1991. Cited on page(s) 70

[31] N. Malpani, J. L. Welch, and N. Vaidya. Leader election algorithms for mobile ad hoc networks. In *Proceedings of the 4th International Workshop on Discrete Algorithms and Methods for Mobile Computing and Communications (DIAL M)*, pages 96–103, 2000. DOI: 10.1145/345848.345871 Cited on page(s) 2, 44

[32] M. Naimi and M. Trehel. An improvement of the $\log n$ distributed algorithm for mutual exclusion. In *Proceedings of the 7th IEEE International Conference on Distributed Computing Systems (ICDCS)*, pages 371–377, 1987. DOI: 10.1109/ICIT.2008.51 Cited on page(s) 46, 59

[33] M. Naimi, M. Trehel, and A. Arnold. A log(n) distributed mutual exclusion algorithm based on path reversal. *Journal of Parallel and Distributed Computing*, 34(1):1–13, 1996. DOI: 10.1006/jpdc.1996.0041 Cited on page(s) 46

[34] M. J. Osborne. *An Introduction to Game Theory*. Oxford University Press, New York, 2003. Cited on page(s) 26

[35] V. D. Park and M. S. Corson. A highly adaptive distributed routing algorithm for mobile wireless networks. In *Proceedings of the 16th IEEE Conference on Computer Communications (IN-FOCOM)*, pages 1405–1413, 1997. DOI: 10.1109/INFCOM.1997.631180 Cited on page(s) 2, 38, 40, 43

[36] T. Radeva. personal communication, 2011. Cited on page(s) 44

[37] T. Radeva and N. A. Lynch. Brief announcement: Partial reversal acyclicity. In *Proceedings of the 30th ACM Symposium on Principles of Distributed Computing (PODC)*, pages 353–354, 2011. DOI: 10.1145/1993806.1993880 Cited on page(s) 18

[38] K. Raymond. A tree-based algorithm for distributed mutual exclusion. *ACM Transactions on Computer Systems*, 7(1):61–77, 1989. DOI: 10.1145/58564.59295 Cited on page(s) 2, 46, 47, 59

[39] G. Tel. *Introduction to Distributed Algorithms, Second Edition*. Cambridge University Press, 2000. Cited on page(s) 44, 45

[40] J. van de Snepscheut. Fair mutual exclusion on a graph of processes. *Distributed Computing*, 2:113–115, 1987. DOI: 10.1007/BF01667083 Cited on page(s) 2, 46, 47, 59

[41] J. Walter, G. Cao, and M. Mohanty. A K-mutual exclusion algorithm for wireless ad-hoc networks. In *Proceedings of the 2001 Workshop on Principles of Mobile Computing (POMC)*, pages 1–11, 2001. Cited on page(s) 87

[42] J. Walter, J. L. Welch, and N. Vaidya. A mutual exclusion algorithm for ad hoc mobile networks. *Wireless Networks*, 7(6):585–600, 2001. DOI: 10.1023/A:1012363200403 Cited on page(s) 2, 47, 56, 57

Authors' Biographies

JENNIFER WELCH

Jennifer Welch received her Ph.D. in Computer Science from MIT in 1988. She is currently a professor in the Department of Computer Science and Engineering at Texas A&M University. She has published numerous technical papers on the theory of distributed computing, is a coauthor on a textbook, has served on the program committees for several international conferences, and is currently a member of the editorial board for the journal *Distributed Computing*. Her research interests include algorithms and lower bounds for distributed computing systems, in particular mobile and wireless networks, and distributed shared objects.

JENNIFER E. WALTER

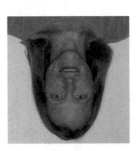

Jennifer E. Walter received her Ph.D. from Texas A&M University in 2000. She is currently an associate professor and Chair of the Computer Science Department at Vassar College. Her research involves the development and simulation of distributed algorithms for mobile ad hoc networks and self-reconfigurable robotic systems.

Printed in the United States
by Baker & Taylor Publisher Services